POEMS OF
PERCY BYSSHE SHELLEY

THE CROWELL POETS

Under the editorship of Lillian Morrison

POEMS OF WILLIAM BLAKE
Selected by Amelia H. Munson

POEMS OF ROBERT BROWNING
Selected by Rosemary Sprague

POEMS OF ROBERT BURNS
Selected by Lloyd Frankenberg

POEMS OF SAMUEL TAYLOR COLERIDGE
Selected by Babette Deutsch

POEMS OF STEPHEN CRANE
Selected by Gerald D. McDonald

POEMS OF EMILY DICKINSON
Selected by Helen Plotz

POEMS OF RALPH WALDO EMERSON
Selected by J. Donald Adams

POEMS OF W. S. GILBERT
Selected by William Cole

POEMS OF ROBERT HERRICK
Selected by Winfield Townley Scott

POEMS OF JOHN KEATS
Selected by Stanley Kunitz

POEMS OF HENRY WADSWORTH
LONGFELLOW
Selected by Edmund Fuller

POEMS OF EDGAR ALLAN POE
Selected by Dwight Macdonald

POEMS OF WILLIAM SHAKESPEARE
Selected by Lloyd Frankenberg

POEMS OF PERCY BYSSHE SHELLEY
Selected by Leo Gurko

POEMS OF ALFRED, LORD TENNYSON
Selected by Ruth Greiner Rausen

POEMS OF WALT WHITMAN
Selected by Lawrence Clark Powell

POEMS OF WILLIAM WORDSWORTH
Selected by Elinor Parker

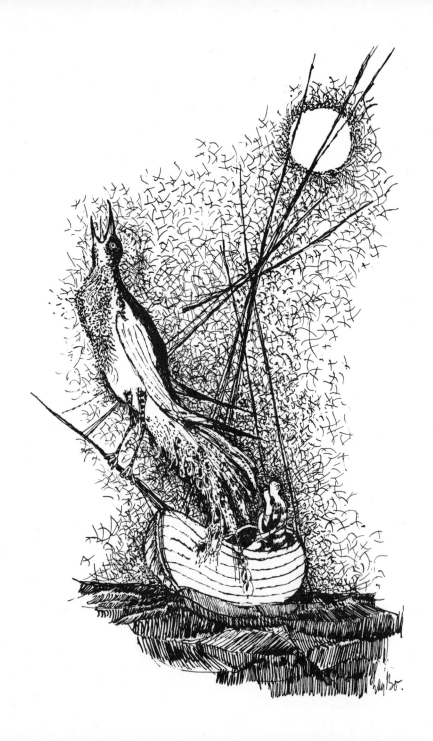

POEMS OF PERCY BYSSHE SHELLEY

Selected by Leo Gurko

Drawings by Lars Bo

THOMAS Y. CROWELL COMPANY: NEW YORK

CONTENTS

I am the eye with which the Universe
    Beholds itself and knows itself divine;
All harmony of instrument or verse,
    All prophecy, all medicine is mine,
All light of art or nature . . . .

—"HYMN OF APOLLO"

AN UNCOMPROMISING SPIRIT

"In everything any man ever wrote, spoke, acted, or imagined, is contained, as it were, an allegorical idea of his own future life, as the acorn contains the oak."
Letter to Thomas Love Peacock, May 2, 1820

The poems of Shelley are a supreme expression of the romantic movement to which he belonged. This was equally true of his life. It had a few marvelously ecstatic moments and long stretches of gloomy melancholy. Shelley was at bitter odds with the conventions of his time and was forced to live his last years in exile because his opinions and personal conduct scandalized his English contemporaries. In politics he was an extreme radical, urging the poor of Europe to rise against their oppressors. He was also a utopian, dreaming of a glorious future in which all men would live together in equality, brotherhood, and peace. He wore a ring with the motto *Il buon tempo verrà*—"the good time will come."

His existence was marked by violently held opinions, a temperament that veered in mood from one extreme of emotion to another, a conviction that life was essentially a war between himself and the world, and a passionate desire to fulfill himself as both a poet and a man. These

I

qualities were shared in greater or lesser degree by Byron and Keats, Shelley's romantic contemporaries, and by Wordsworth and Coleridge in their younger days. They were political and intellectual radicals, who believed in the inevitable conflict between society and the individual, and stressed the fulfillment of personal genius.

Percy Bysshe Shelley was born in 1792, four years after Byron and three before Keats. He was the son of a well-to-do gentleman farmer in Sussex and the grandson of a wealthy baronet. He grew up idolized by four younger sisters. He was exceptionally good looking, with curly hair and a delicate, almost girlish complexion. By the time he went off to school, he was used to having his own way and got into trouble at once by refusing to conform to the practices of his schoolfellows. He was bored by organized games and at Eton refused to take part in the tradition of performing menial services for the senior boys. As a result he was jeered at and bullied. This made no difference to Shelley. He stood his ground, fought back as best he could, and though often humiliated and reduced to tears, refused to give in. He felt that he had a right to his own opinions and to behave as he chose, and that no one else had the right to take these freedoms away from him.

When he entered Oxford in the fall of 1810, Shelley demanded unrestricted freedom to think, speak, and write as he pleased. This soon involved him in difficulties with the college authorities. He and a fellow classmate,

Thomas Jefferson Hogg, published and circulated an anonymous pamphlet called *The Necessity of Atheism.* They were summoned before a board of inquiry headed by the dean, and asked whether they were the authors. Shelley refused to answer on the grounds that his rights were being violated, and was promptly expelled. Hogg freely admitted his share in the pamphlet and was also expelled. In the spring of 1811 the two youths went down to London and took a scrubby room in Poland Street. Poland was one of the countries then struggling for its independence against the empires of Russia and Prussia, and Shelley thought the name of the street symbolically apt.

Shelley's father, a man of mildly liberal opinions and a Whig member of Parliament, was furious. He advised his son to recant his atheism, apologize to the dean, and restore himself to the good graces of the community. Shelley refused. This was the beginning of a long quarrel with his father that was to lead to their permanent estrangement and cost Shelley most of his inheritance.

At eighteen his ideas were already formed. He was a revolutionary in politics, an atheist in religion, and a vegetarian in diet. He had read, thoroughly absorbed, and been deeply influenced by the radical tracts of the day: Tom Paine's *The Rights of Man,* William Godwin's *Political Justice,* the skeptical philosophy of David Hume, and the works of Rousseau. Shelley regarded the French Revolution as the sacred event of his era, an event betrayed by Napoleon with whom England was now at war. But the British government, Tory, reactionary, repressive of free speech and publication, headed by the formidable younger Pitt, was also anathema to Shelley. He was against the war, not out of sympathy for Napoleon, but because he was against all war, which he regarded as a plot by the ruling classes to distract the oppressed peoples from their misery. He was against kings, aristocrats, and priests, and dreamed of the glorious days in the future when all men would be economically and politically equal. He regarded the United States as a model republic and was outraged when England declared war on her former colony in 1812. In all these attitudes Shelley was absolutely uncompromising. He was without doubt the most inflexible, I-shall-die-at-the-stake-for-my-principles idealist in English literature.

He had equally strong ideas about personal conduct and morals. Taking his cue from Godwin and from Godwin's first wife, Mary Wollstonecraft, the famous crusading feminist, Shelley regarded marriage as still another form of enslavement. A man and woman should live together as long as they were in love. When they fell out of love, they should be free to separate. To be forced to remain together lovelessly by the formal requirements of matrimony was, to Shelley, a hell on earth, a terrible bondage, another chain by which society sought to hamper individual freedom. In one of his famous love poems, *Epipsychidion* (Greek for "a soul within the soul"), he expresses his doctrine of free love in the passage beginning with the line, "I never was attached to that great sect." Shelley's support of this doctrine was another point of painful friction between himself and the public opinion of his day. Nevertheless, like Godwin before him, he married twice, justifying his actions in each case by saying that, the world being what it was, the price paid by the woman in loss of reputation was too cruel to be borne. These were among the few occasions when Shelley was willing to compromise his principles.

His difficulties with his father increased when in the fall of 1811 he eloped with Harriet Westbrook, the sixteen-year-old daughter of a well-to-do retired tavernkeeper. Shelley was only nineteen. His father felt he was too young and that he had married beneath him. But parental opposition had no effect on Shelley. He was determined to mold Harriet's mind after his own and at the same time to reform the world. Accompanied by Harriet's older sister, the newlyweds journeyed to Dublin where Shelley wrote and distributed pamphlets urging the subjugated Irish to demand their independence from England. Nothing much came of this, and the young Shelleys returned to England in 1812. Shelley now began bombarding the authorities with open letters and broadsides demanding freedom for persons being prosecuted by the regime for sedition. He contributed out of his own meagre income to scores of radical and humanitarian causes, including an ambitious project to settle poor people upon land reclaimed from the sea. And he at last met the man whom he had idolized since first reading his famous book on political justice, William Godwin.

Godwin craved two things from the world: money and adulation. Shelley was eager to supply both. Of admiration for Godwin's intellect, Shelley had an unlimited supply. To him, Godwin was one of the great minds of the age, the guide and molder of his own political life. Money, however, was in short supply, and heavy demands were being made on what little he had. Godwin, a bad businessman, was perpetually in debt and had no scruples about taking money from Shelley, or for that matter from any of the disciples who came to pay their respects. Shelley gave him sums of ready cash when these were available and borrowed, at shocking rates of interest, against the estate he expected one day to inherit from his father, to plug up Godwin's leaky finances.

At Godwin's house, in addition to rich intellectual conversation joined in by Coleridge, Lamb, Hazlitt, and other celebrated visitors, Shelley found one other supreme attraction, Godwin's seventeen-year-old daughter Mary. Shelley's relationship with Harriet had already begun to cool, and he was ready to fall in love with someone else. Mary was young, pretty, highly intelligent, and very willing to be in love with Shelley. In 1814 the two of them, accompanied by Claire Clairmont, daughter of Godwin's second wife by a previous marriage, ran off to the Continent. Godwin, despite his advanced theories about free love, was furious. Godwin the father was very different from Godwin the philosopher. He led the scandalized outcry that arose in England against Shelley, now accused of being a seducer and abandoner of wife and child (Harriet at this time was expecting their second baby), as well as a bloodthirsty radical.

The next four years were fantastically troubled and complicated. The "elopement" with Mary outraged Shelley's father, who placed further difficulties in the way of his income and eventual inheritance. Mary bore him a child out of wedlock, but it died a few weeks after birth. After being deserted by Shelley, Harriet sank into an acute depression that grew progressively worse; in the end she drowned herself. Immediately after Harriet's death, Shelley married Mary, but despite this gesture toward respectability the court denounced him as unfit to be a father and removed his two children by Harriet from his care. Two more children were born to Shelley and Mary during this period, and Shelley feared that the authorities would snatch them from him as well. All the while he was harried by Godwin, by Harriet's father and sister, by his own extravagant generosity, and by the disturbed political climate marked by the resurgence of reactionary governments in Europe and England after the defeat of Napoleon.

But it was not all melancholy. There were intervals of

very real enjoyment and happiness. Shelley, Mary, and Claire spent the summer of 1816 in Switzerland and there met Byron, the most popular and renowned poet of the day, famous for his radical opinions and his lurid love affairs. The two poets got along from the start, each admiring in the other the qualities lacking in himself. Shelley was fascinated by Byron's brilliant conversation, sophisticated manners, and air of cynical bravado. Byron, in turn, was impressed by Shelley's idealism, his purity of motive, his reckless benevolence, and his sincere indifference to what others thought of him. Shelley is the Julian and Byron the Count Maddalo of Shelley's later poem *Julian and Maddalo*, which describes the relationship between them. Another of Shelley's close friends was Leigh Hunt, the liberal editor and poet, whose good temper and genial spirits made his house in Hampstead a center for the young writers of the day. It was there that Shelley met John Keats.

All this time he was writing poetry. As a boy his juvenile poems had run to wizards and demons. When he became socially conscious, his poetry used the events of the day as springboards for his outraged emotions over injustice and exploitation and for his fiery optimism about the revolutionary future. The earliest mature effort along these lines was *Queen Mab*, a long ramble through history, past, present, and future, in which Shelley violently condemns his own age and first establishes in a major poem his special blend of private feeling and social argument. The period of deepening unhappiness and personal disturbance between 1814 and 1818 was reflected in a long, semiautobiographical poem, *Alastor*, the tale of a young poet much like Shelley who travels through exotic landscapes all over the world looking for an ideal human embodiment of his dreams. He does not find it, and ends shriveling in the isolation of his private self.

Unlike the hero of *Alastor*, Shelley did not shrivel under the deliberately self-made difficulties of his life. Though he was given to fits of depression, he also had many periods of cheerfulness and ebullience. He responded to trouble with remarkable resilience, supported always by his unflinching optimism about the future of human society and by his Platonic belief that all experiences and emotions had their ideal forms which, freed from the imperfections of the physical world, could delight the mind. Shelley read Plato in the original, as he did all the Greek and Roman writers. In addition to Greek and Latin, he had also mastered French, Italian, Spanish, and German. He read widely in all these languages, and when not actually working on his own poems would translate the works of foreign writers. With the exception of Milton, Shelley was probably the most learned of the English poets.

He was also one of the most intellectually curious. Literature and politics were not his only interests. He was almost equally attracted to religion, philosophy, and science. Astronomy, in particular, was an early passion of Shelley's. From it he derived a fascination for the element of air. Byron's poetry is filled with references to water, Wordsworth's to earth. Shelley's special element was the air and all things ethereal. His poems are saturated with stars, clouds, mist, hail, wind, storm, and rain. He is always on the wing, whether through the actual physical ether as in "Ode to the West Wind," "To a Skylark," or "The Cloud," or through the metaphysical ether of future time, the great future that beckoned mankind, as in *Queen Mab* and *Prometheus Unbound*. "As to real flesh & blood," he wrote to John Gisborne, "you know that I do not deal in these articles,—you might as well go to a gin-shop for a leg of mutton, as expect anything human or earthly from me."

But Shelley was not only a Platonist. He was also an anti-Platonist. He was engrossed by the idea of perfection, in love, in politics, and in poetry; at the same time he was intoxicated by sensuous objects in a state of change and metamorphosis. The hero of *Alastor*—a poem that can be read as a warning against Plato—withers away when he becomes too removed from life and the living world, too absorbed in ideals. Yet the ideal goals of life and love are the pre-eminent themes in all of Shelley's poems that deal, literally (*Hellas*) or metaphorically (*Prometheus Unbound*), with social revolution. For all his tendency to career off toward the extremes, he did embrace a fusion of sense and spirit, and never allowed one to be negated by the other. In this respect his debt to the ancient Greeks, with their dream of harmony and balance, was incalculable, a debt he enthusiastically acknowledged in his remark, "We are all Greeks."

By 1818 Shelley's position in England had become intolerable. He was out of favor with nearly everyone: his father, his father-in-law, Harriet's relatives, the courts, and his numerous creditors. The government dominated by Lord Castlereagh looked upon him, quite rightly, as a dangerous enemy. He was reviled as a ravisher of women, a subverter of convention, and a seditionist against the state. Shelley had his friends and admirers, but they were not influential enough to control or subdue the outcries against him. In 1818 he and Mary, accompanied by their two children and the ever-present Claire, left England for Italy. Shelley was never to return.

Italy was a relief from England, and its sensuous landscape stimulated Shelley to write his most beautiful lyric poems. But he was also lonely there, suffering not just from social isolation but from a conviction that his works were unread and his voice unheard. The Shelleys wandered restlessly from city to city. They began in Florence, then moved to Venice where their daughter Clara died. Then to Rome, where their son William died.

Then to Naples and finally Pisa. Haggard with grief, they found some solace in Pisa with the arrival of their fourth child, Percy, the only one who did survive, and through a circle of friends and acquaintances, including Byron, that enriched the last eighteen months of Shelley's life.

The Italian period saw the creation of his greatest poems. He wrote *Prometheus Unbound*, an immense four-act lyrical drama about the heroic refusal of Prometheus to give in to the tyranny of Jupiter. Shelley reacted to the death of Keats in 1821 with the famous elegy *Adonais*, a poem that expressed as much of Shelley's personal hostility to the critics who had abused both himself and Keats as it did his admiration for Keats's genius and his belief in Keats's immortality. It was in Italy, appropriately, that he composed *The Cenci*, his one play intended for the stage, dealing with the bloody actions of a Renaissance tyrant who at last, though at heavy cost, is overthrown.

While staying for a time at the Italian villa of some English friends, the Gisbornes, Shelley, puttering about the workshop of the Gisbornes' son Henry, an inventor, was moved to write in rhyming couplets the charming "Letter to Maria Gisborne," in which he expresses his sense of the friendship between them and his pleasure at tinkering with mechanical objects. His interest in scientific inventions and mechanical contraptions went back to his childhood and his months at college. His rooms at

Oxford were always cluttered with the latest gadgets and odds and ends of experiments in physics and chemistry. Shelley took justifiable pride in his scientific knowledge, a knowledge reflected in a number of his poems. "The Cloud," for example, is not only a beautiful lyric but, unlike many English nature poems, is also scrupulously accurate in its dazzling descriptions of the phenomena of weather.

Pisa was also the scene of his indulgence in what Mary called "Shelley's Italian platonics." He fell in love with a beautiful Italian girl named Emilia Viviani, confined against her will to a convent by her stepmother. Under the stimulus of this emotion he wrote a number of fervently eloquent love poems to her. Later, the Shelleys shared a villa on the Ligurian coast with a young English couple, Edward and Jane Williams. Shelley promptly fell in love with Jane and composed a number of throbbing lyrics to her, including the memorable *With a Guitar: To Jane.*

Meanwhile he remained alert to every political upheaval in Europe. A republican uprising in Spain inspired his "Ode to Liberty." A republican uprising in Naples inspired his "Ode to Naples." An uprising of the Greeks against the Turkish occupiers stirred him to write *Hellas.* In his last years poetry became his only form of social action. Indeed, he was at last persuaded that poetry was a superior mode of action. In a magnificent essay, "A Defence of Poetry," he argued that poets were not only figures of singular power but that they were "the un-acknowledged legislators of the world."

The villa on the Bay of Spezia shared by the Shelleys and the Williamses was Shelley's last home. He had a passion for sailing, and moved from Pisa to the coast in order to indulge it freely. Williams was also an enthusiastic sailor, and the two men would spend hours, sometimes days, on the water. For all his love of the sea, Shelley never learned to swim. Byron, a powerful swimmer, tried to teach him, but Shelley, out of some obscure fatalism, refused to learn. He also refused to be taught by Edward Trelawney, a romantic Welsh adventurer who became an intimate part of Shelley's circle during the poet's last year. With great enthusiasm Shelley commissioned a boat for himself and Williams to be built by a seagoing friend of Trelawney's. He called it the *Don Juan*, as a tribute to Byron's poem of the same name.

In it the two friends embarked on their last journey. It was July 1822. They sailed to Leghorn to meet Leigh Hunt, whom Shelley had invited down from England to edit a new literary-radical magazine to which he and Byron would contribute. After several days of discussion Shelley and Williams, accompanied by an English youth helping them with the boat, started for home. A storm was blowing up in the bay, and Shelley was warned to postpone the trip. He and Williams, however, were anxious to return to their wives. Trelawney, seriously alarmed, watched them through binoculars as they left the harbor. In the distance he saw the squall blow up, darkening the sea. The boat disappeared into it and was seen no more. By an uncanny coincidence Shelley anticipated the details of his death in the last stanza of *Adonais*.

Three days later the bodies were washed ashore. Shelley's remains were cremated on the beach. During the ceremony, Trelawney suddenly thrust his hand into the fire and plucked out Shelley's heart. Ashes and heart were later buried in the Protestant Cemetery in Rome near the graves of Keats and of Shelley's young son William. The poet, just short of his thirtieth year, died far from England, an exile in death as in life.

Keats had died in Rome the year before; Byron was to die in Greece two years later. Shelley represented that generation of romantic poets in its purest form. It stood for a break with the past, for youth as against the aging rulers of the day, for moral and sexual freedom as against convention, for a new world and a new social order as against the old. It was young, ardent, naïve, egotistical, and immensely self-conscious.

All these qualities, in an extreme, often wildly exaggerated form, are visible in Shelley. His poems are driven by an extraordinary energy. They may at times be undisciplined, verbally inflated, and irritatingly repetitive, but they are always animated. The movement of his verse is restless, the tone feverish. Shelley once said to Trelawney, "When my brain gets heated with thought, it soon boils, and throws off images and words faster than I can skim them off." Shelley's images and words rush at the reader in unflagging pulsations, exactly reflecting the poet's temperament and even his social manner. Vigor, mobility, and a hard-driving, relentless insistence on being heard dominate his work. And just as his personal life oscillated between ecstatic buoyancy and fits of depression, so his poems range from deep melancholy to soaring ecstasy, with scarcely a pause between. Among the major English poets, Shelley is the great specialist in these emotions. This intensity of feeling was accompanied and to some extent controlled by a remarkable lyric sense. Shelley's verse is filled not only with emotion but with song. Reading aloud the choruses from *Hellas*, or the fragments "When Soft Winds and Sunny Skies" and "Wine of the Fairies," or the opening three stanzas of "Ode to the West Wind" provides a vibrant demonstration of Shelley's musical powers.

He addresses us today as both poet and prophet. Early in life he had come to an absolute judgment of the upper-class English world into which he was born: he rejected it and was one of the early avowers of passive resistance to it. He was indeed a famous apostle of passive resistance, a forerunner of Thoreau, Gandhi, and in our own immediate day, Martin Luther King. "If the tyrants command their troops to fire upon the people," he wrote in "A Philosophical View of Reform," "or cut them down unless they disperse, the true patriot will exhort them peaceably to risk the danger, and to expect without resistance the onset of the cavalry, and wait with folded arms the fire of the artillery, and receive with unshrinking bosoms the bayonets of the charging battalions."

That other side of Shelley, his love of argument and defense of rationality, made George Bernard Shaw one of his greatest admirers. Yet Shelley's attitudes were singularly oversimplified, and he would have been classified by sophisticated radicals of the twentieth century as an infantile leftist. He thought, naïvely and defiantly, that all politicians and priests—up to and including, as he insisted, God Himself—were wicked and that the masses of people were automatically innocent victims of oppression. He assumed that kings and aristocrats, without exception, were automatically the enemies of virtue and justice; that the present, bad as it was, was better than the past; and that the future, as yet uncreated, was certain to be better still. His belief in the idea of progress was as stubbornly positive as his polarized view of the world as a whole.

He was more widely condemned than read in his own day, but with each generation since his death his vilifiers diminished and his readers increased. His poems, with their passionately expressed emotions and exquisite utopian visions of an ideal future, make their ardent and moving appeal to us amid the oppressive difficulties of our own age.

·I·
THE CORRUPT
PRESENT AND THE
VISIONARY FUTURE

". . . I have, what a Scotch philosopher characteristically terms, 'a passion for reforming the world'. . . ."

—PREFACE TO *Prometheus Unbound*

Ozymandias

I met a traveller from an antique land
Who said: Two vast and trunkless legs of stone
Stand in the desert. Near them, on the sand,
Half sunk, a shattered visage lies, whose frown,
And wrinkled lip, and sneer of cold command,
Tell that its sculptor well those passions read
Which yet survive, stamped on these lifeless things,
The hand that mocked them, and the heart that fed;
And on the pedestal these words appear:
"My name is Ozymandias, king of kings:
Look on my works, ye Mighty, and despair!"
Nothing beside remains. Round the decay
Of that colossal wreck, boundless and bare
The lone and level sands stretch far away.

Song to the Men of England

1

Men of England, wherefore plough
For the lords who lay ye low?
Wherefore weave with toil and care,
The rich robes your tyrants wear?

2

Wherefore feed, and clothe, and save,
From the cradle to the grave,
Those ungrateful drones who would
Drain your sweat—nay, drink your blood?

3

Wherefore, Bees of England, forge
Many a weapon, chain, and scourge,
That these stingless drones may spoil
The forced produce of your toil?

4

Have ye leisure, comfort, calm,
Shelter, food, love's gentle balm?
Or what is it ye buy so dear
With your pain and with your fear?

5

The seed ye sow, another reaps;
The wealth ye find, another keeps;
The robes ye weave, another wears;
The arms ye forge, another bears.

6

Sow seed,—but let no tyrant reap;
Find wealth,—let no impostor heap;
Weave robes,—let not the idle wear;
Forge arms,—in your defence to bear.

7

Shrink to your cellars, holes, and cells;
In halls ye deck, another dwells.
Why shake the chains ye wrought? Ye see
The steel ye tempered glance on ye.

8

With plough and spade, and hoe and loom,
Trace your grave, and build your tomb.
And weave your winding-sheet, till fair
England be your sepulchre.

England in 1819

An old, mad, blind, despised, and dying king,—
Princes, the dregs of their dull race, who flow
Through public scorn—mud from a muddy spring;
Rulers, who neither see, nor feel, nor know,
But leech-like to their fainting country cling,
Till they drop, blind in blood, without a blow;
A people starved and stabbed in the untilled field,—
An army, which liberticide and prey
Makes as a two-edged sword to all who wield—
Golden and sanguine laws which tempt and slay,—
Religion Christless, Godless—a book sealed;
A Senate,—Time's worst statute unrepealed,—
Are graves, from which a glorious Phantom may
Burst, to illumine our tempestuous day.

Fragment: "Alas! This Is Not What I Thought Life Was"

Alas! this is not what I thought life was.
I knew that there were crimes and evil men,
Misery and hate; nor did I hope to pass
Untouched by suffering, through the rugged glen.
In mine own heart I saw as in a glass
The hearts of others.   And when
I went among my kind, with triple brass
Of calm endurance my weak breast I armed,
To bear scorn, fear, and hate, a woful mass!

from Hellas

Chorus

In the great morning of the world,
The spirit of God with might unfurl'd
The flag of Freedom over Chaos,
   And all its banded anarchs fled,
Like vultures frighted from Imaus,
   Before an earthquake's tread.—
So from Time's tempestuous dawn

Freedom's splendour burst and shone:—
Thermopylae and Marathon
Caught, like mountains beacon-lighted,
    The springing Fire.—The wingèd glory
On Philippi half-alighted,
    Like an eagle on a promontory.
Its unwearied wings could fan
The quenchless ashes of Milan.
From age to age, from man to man,
    It lived; and lit from land to land
    Florence, Albion, Switzerland.

Then night fell; and, as from night,
Re-assuming fiery flight,
From the West swift freedom came,
    Against the course of heaven and doom,
A second sun array'd in flame,
    To burn, to kindle, to illume.
From far Atlantis its young beams
Chased the shadows and the dreams.
France, with all her sanguine steams,
    Hid, but quench'd it not; again
    Through clouds its shafts of glory rain
    From utmost Germany to Spain.

As an eagle fed with morning
Scorns the embattled tempest's warning,
When she seeks her aerie hanging
    In the mountain-cedar's hair,

And her brood expect the clanging
  Of her wings through the wild air,
Sick with famine:—Freedom, so
To what of Greece remaineth now
Returns; her hoary ruins glow
Like orient mountains lost in day;
  Beneath the safety of her wings
Her renovated nurslings prey,
  And in the naked lightnings
Of truth they purge their dazzled eyes.
Let Freedom leave, where'er she flies,
A Desert, or a Paradise;
  Let the beautiful and the brave
  Share her glory, or a grave.

                (lines 46–93)

Chorus

Worlds on worlds are rolling ever
  From creation to decay,
Like the bubbles on a river
  Sparkling, bursting, borne away.
  But they are still immortal
  Who, through birth's orient portal
And death's dark chasm hurrying to and fro,
  Clothe their unceasing flight
  In the brief dust and light
Gather'd around their chariots as they go;

New shapes they still may weave,
New Gods, new laws receive,
Bright or dim are they, as the robes they last
On Death's bare ribs had cast.

A power from the unknown God;
A Promethean conqueror, came;
Like a triumphal path he trod
The thorns of death and shame.
A mortal shape to him
Was like the vapour dim
Which the orient planet animates with light.

(lines 197–217)

Semichorus I

Let the tyrants rule the desert they have made;
Let the free possess the Paradise they claim;
Be the fortune of our fierce oppressors weighed
With our ruin, our resistance, and our name!

Semichorus II

Our dead shall be the seed of their decay,
Our survivors be the shadow of their pride,
Our adversity a dream to pass away,—
Their dishonour a remembrance to abide!

(lines 1008–1015)

Chorus

The world's great age begins anew,
    The golden years return,
The earth doth like a snake renew
    Her winter weeds outworn:
Heaven smiles, and faiths and empires gleam,
Like wrecks of a dissolving dream.

A brighter Hellas rears its mountains
    From waves serener far;
A new Peneus rolls his fountains
    Against the morning-star.
Where fairer Tempes bloom, there sleep
Young Cyclads on a sunnier deep.

A loftier Argo cleaves the main,
    Fraught with a later prize;
Another Orpheus sings again,
    And loves, and weeps, and dies.
A new Ulysses leaves once more
Calypso for his native shore.

                (lines 1060–1077)

O cease! must hate and death return?
    Cease! must men kill and die?

Cease! drain not to its dregs the urn
    Of bitter prophecy.
The world is weary of the past,
O might it die or rest at last!

(lines 1096–1101)

Fragment: Milton's Spirit

I dreamed that Milton's spirit rose, and took
    From life's green tree his Uranian lute;
And from his touch sweet thunder flowed, and shook
All human things built in contempt of man,—
And sanguine thrones and impious altars quaked,
Prisons and citadels . . .

Sonnet

Lift not the painted veil which those who live
Call Life: though unreal shapes be pictured there,
And it but mimic all we would believe
With colours idly spread,—behind, lurk Fear
And Hope, twin Destinies; who ever weave
Their shadows, o'er the chasm, sightless and drear.
I knew one who had lifted it—he sought,
For his lost heart was tender, things to love,
But found them not, alas! nor was there aught
The world contains, the which he could approve.
Through the unheeding many he did move,
A splendour among shadows, a bright blot
Upon this gloomy scene, a Spirit that strove
For truth, and like the Preacher found it not.

from Prometheus Unbound

The poem deals with the refusal of Prometheus to accept the tyrannical authority of Jupiter, king of the gods. Prometheus endures endless torture and humiliation, but does not submit. Asia, his bride, summons Demogorgon to the rescue. Demogorgon symbolizes historical necessity, a force which is blind unless guided by love, represented in the poem by Asia. Demogorgon overthrows Jupiter and frees Prometheus. The liberated hero then describes the visionary future to the nymphs who have come to celebrate his freedom. Later, other spirits report on changes already taking place in the hearts of men.

Asia

My soul is an enchanted boat,
   Which, like a sleeping swan, doth float
Upon the silver waves of thy sweet singing;
   And thine doth like an angel sit
   Beside a helm conducting it,
Whilst all the winds with melody are ringing.
   It seems to float ever, for ever,
   Upon that many-winding river,
   Between mountains, woods, abysses,
   A paradise of wildernesses!
Till, like one in slumber bound,

Borne to the ocean, I float down, around,
Into a sea profound, of ever-spreading sound:

Meanwhile thy spirit lifts its pinions
In music's most serene dominions:
Catching the winds that fan that happy heaven.
And we sail on, away, afar,
Without a course, without a star,
But, by the instinct of sweet music driven;
Till through Elysian garden islets
By thee, most beautiful of pilots,
Where never mortal pinnace glided,
The boat of my desire is guided:
Realms where the air we breathe is love,
Which in the winds and on the waves doth move,
Harmonizing this earth with what we feel above.

We have passed Age's icy caves,
And Manhood's dark and tossing waves,
And Youth's smooth ocean, smiling to betray:
Beyond the glassy gulfs we flee
Of shadow-peopled Infancy,
Through Death and Birth, to a diviner day;
A paradise of vaulted bowers
Lit by downward-gazing flowers,
And watery paths that wind between
Wildernesses calm and green,
Peopled by shapes too bright to see,

And rest, having beheld; somewhat like thee;
Which walk upon the sea, and chant melodiously!
(Act II, scene 5, lines 71–110)

  Prometheus.   . . . There is a cave,
All overgrown with trailing odorous plants,
Which curtain out the day with leaves and flowers,
And paved with veinèd emerald, and a fountain
Leaps in the midst with an awakening sound.
From its curved roof the mountain's frozen tears,
Like snow, or silver, or long diamond spires,
Hang downward, raining forth a doubtful light:
And there is heard the ever-moving air,
Whispering without from tree to tree, and birds,
And bees; and all around are mossy seats,
And the rough walls are clothed with long soft grass;
A simple dwelling, which shall be our own;
Where we will sit and talk of time and change,
As the world ebbs and flows, ourselves unchanged.
What can hide man from mutability?
And if ye sigh, then I will smile; and thou,
Ione, shalt chant fragments of sea-music,
Until I weep, when ye shall smile away
The tears she brought, which yet were sweet to shed.
We will entangle buds and flowers and beams
Which twinkle on the fountain's brim, and make

Strange combinations out of common things,
Like human babes in their brief innocence;
And we will search, with looks and words of love,
For hidden thoughts, each lovelier than the last,
Our unexhausted spirits; and like lutes
Touched by the skill of the enamoured wind,
Weave harmonies divine, yet ever new,
From difference sweet where discord cannot be;
And hither come, sped on the charmèd winds,
Which meet from all the points of heaven, as bees
From every flower aërial Enna feeds,
At their known island-homes in Himera,
The echoes of the human world, which tell
Of the low voice of love, almost unheard,
And dove-eyed pity's murmured pain, and music,
Itself the echo of the heart, and all
That tempers or improves man's life, now free;
And lovely apparitions,—dim at first,
Then radiant, as the mind, arising bright
From the embrace of beauty, whence the forms
Of which these are the phantoms, casts on them
The gathered rays which are reality,
Shall visit us, the progeny immortal
Of Painting, Sculpture, and rapt Poesy,
And arts, tho' unimagined, yet to be.
The wandering voices and the shadows these
Of all that man becomes, the mediators

Of that best worship love, by him and us
Given and returned; swift shapes and sounds, which
    grow
More fair and soft as man grows wise and kind,
And veil by veil, evil and error fall:
Such virtue has the cave and place around.

                    (Act III, scene 3, lines 10–63)

   Spirit of the Earth. Thou knowest that toads, and
       snakes, and loathly worms,
And venomous and malicious beasts, and boughs
That bore ill berries in the woods, were ever
An hindrance to my walks o'er the green world:
And that, among the haunts of humankind,
Hard-featured men, or with proud angry looks,
Or cold, staid gait, or false and hollow smiles,
Or the dull sneer of self-loved ignorance,
Or other such foul masks, with which ill thoughts
Hide that fair being whom we spirits call man;
And women too, ugliest of all things evil,
(Tho' fair, even in a world where thou art fair,
When good and kind, free and sincere like thee),
When false or frowning made me sick at heart
To pass them, tho' they slept, and I unseen.
Well, my path lately lay thro' a great city
Into the woody hills surrounding it:

A sentinel was sleeping at the gate:
When there was heard a sound, so loud, it shook
The towers amid the moonlight, yet more sweet
Than any voice but thine, sweetest of all;
A long, long sound, as it would never end:
And all the inhabitants leapt suddenly
Out of their rest, and gathered in the streets,
Looking in wonder up to Heaven, while yet
The music pealed along. I hid myself
Within a fountain in the public square,
Where I lay like the reflex of the moon
Seen in a wave under green leaves; and soon
Those ugly human shapes and visages
Of which I spoke as having wrought me pain,
Passed floating thro' the air, and fading still
Into the winds that scattered them; and those
From whom they passed seemed mild and lovely forms
After some foul disguise had fallen, and all
Were somewhat changed, and after a brief surprise
And greetings of delighted wonder, all
Went to their sleep again: and when the dawn
Came, would'st thou think that toads, and snakes, and
    efts,
Could e'er be beautiful? yet so they were,
And that with little change of shape or hue:
All things had put their evil nature off.

(Act III, scene 4, lines 36–77)

   Spirit of the Hour. . . . but soon I looked,
And behold, thrones were kingless, and men walked
One with the other even as spirits do,
None fawned, none trampled; hate, disdain, or fear,
Self-love or self-contempt, on human brows
No more inscribed, as o'er the gate of hell,
"All hope abandon ye who enter here;"
None frowned, none trembled, none with eager fear
Gazed on another's eye of cold command,
Until the subject of a tyrant's will
Became, worse fate, the abject of his own,
Which spurred him, like an outspent horse, to death.
None wrought his lips in truth-entangling lines
Which smiled the lie his tongue disdained to speak;
None, with firm sneer, trod out in his own heart
The sparks of love and hope till there remained
Those bitter ashes, a soul self-consumed,
And the wretch crept a vampire among men,
Infecting all with his own hideous ill;
None talked that common, false, cold, hollow talk
Which makes the heart deny the *yes* it breathes,
Yet question that unmeant hypocrisy
With such a self-mistrust as has no name.
And women, too, frank, beautiful, and kind
As the free heaven which rains fresh light and dew
On the wide earth, past; gentle radiant forms,
From custom's evil taint exempt and pure;

Speaking the wisdom once they could not think,
Looking emotions once they feared to feel,
And changed to all which once they dared not be,
Yet being now, made earth like heaven; nor pride,
Nor jealousy, nor envy, nor ill shame,
The bitterest of those drops of treasured gall,
Spoilt the sweet taste of the nepenthe, love.

Thrones, altars, judgment-seats, and prisons; wherein,
And beside which, by wretched men were borne
Sceptres, tiaras, swords, and chains, and tomes
Of reasoned wrong, glozed on by ignorance,
Were like those monstrous and barbaric shapes,
The ghosts of a no-more-remembered fame,
Which, from their unworn obelisks, look forth
In triumph o'er the palaces and tombs
Of those who were their conquerors: mouldering round,
These imaged to the pride of kings and priests,
A dark yet mighty faith, a power as wide
As is the world it wasted, and are now
But an astonishment; even so the tools
And emblems of its last captivity,
Amid the dwellings of the peopled earth,
Stand, not o'erthrown, but unregarded now.
And those foul shapes, abhorred by god and man,—
Which, under many a name and many a form

Strange, savage, ghastly, dark, and execrable,
Were Jupiter, the tyrant of the world;
And which the nations, panic-stricken, served
With blood, and hearts broken by long hope, and love
Dragged to his altars soiled and garlandless,
And slain amid men's unreclaiming tears,
Flattering the thing they feared, which fear was hate,—
Frown, mouldering fast, o'er their abandoned shrines:
The painted veil, by those who were, called life,
Which mimicked, as with colours idly spread,
All men believed or hoped, is torn aside;
The loathesome mask has fallen, the man remains,—
Sceptreless, free, uncircumscribed,—but man:
Equal, unclassed, tribeless and nationless,
Exempt from awe, worship, degree, the king
Over himself; just, gentle, wise;—but man
Passionless?—no, yet free from guilt or pain,
Which were, for his will made or suffered them,
Nor yet exempt, tho' ruling them like slaves,
From chance, and death, and mutability,
The clogs of that which else might oversoar
The loftiest star of unascended heaven,
Pinnacled dim in the intense inane.

(Act III, scene 4, lines 130–204)

Chorus of Spirits and Hours

Then weave the web of the mystic measure;
From the depths of the sky and the ends of the earth,
Come, swift Spirits of might and of pleasure,
Fill the dance and the music of mirth,
As the waves of a thousand streams rush by
To an ocean of splendour and harmony!

(Act IV, scene 1, lines 131–136)

Demogorgon

To suffer woes which Hope thinks infinite;
To forgive wrongs darker than death or night;
To defy Power, which seems omnipotent;
To love, and bear; to hope, till Hope creates
From its own wreck the thing it contemplates:
Neither to change, nor falter, nor repent;
This, like thy glory, Titan! is to be
Good, great and joyous, beautiful and free;
This is alone Life, Joy, Empire, and Victory!

(Act IV, scene 1, lines 572–580)

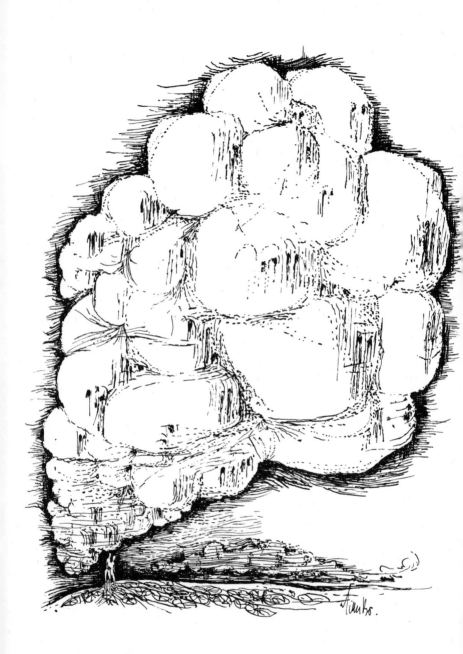

·II·
THE
DAZZLING FACE
OF NATURE

"In the motion of the very leaves of spring, in the blue air, there is then found a secret correspondence with our heart. There is eloquence in the tongueless wind, and a melody in the flowing brooks and the rustling of the reeds beside them, which by their inconceivable relation to something within the soul, awaken the spirits to a dance of breathless rapture, and bring tears of mysterious tenderness to the eyes . . . ."

—"ON LOVE"

The Cloud

I bring fresh showers for the thirsting flowers
    From the seas and the streams;
I bear light shade for the leaves when laid
    In their noon-day dreams.
From my wings are shaken the dews that waken
    The sweet buds every one,
When rocked to rest on their mother's breast,
    As she dances about the sun.
I wield the flail of the lashing hail,
    And whiten the green plains under,
And then again I dissolve it in rain,
    And laugh as I pass in thunder.

I sift the snow on the mountains below,
    And their great pines groan aghast;
And all the night 'tis my pillow white,
    While I sleep in the arms of the blast.
Sublime on the towers of my skiey bowers,
    Lightning my pilot sits;
In a cavern under is fettered the thunder,
    It struggles and howls at fits;
Over earth and ocean, with gentle motion,
    This pilot is guiding me,
Lured by the love of the genii that move
    In the depths of the purple sea;

Over the rills, and the crags, and the hills,
    Over the lakes and the plains,
Wherever he dream, under mountain or stream,
    The Spirit he loves remains;
And I all the while bask in heaven's blue smile,
    Whilst he is dissolving in rains.

The sanguine sunrise, with his meteor eyes,
    And his burning plumes outspread,
Leaps on the back of my sailing rack,
    When the morning star shines dead;
As on the jag of a mountain crag,
    Which an earthquake rocks and swings,
An eagle alit one moment may sit
    In the light of its golden wings.
And when sunset may breathe, from the lit sea beneath,
    Its ardours of rest and of love,
And the crimson pall of eve may fall
    From the depth of heaven above,
With wings folded I rest, on mine airy nest,
    As still as a brooding dove.

That orbèd maiden with white fire laden,
    Whom mortals call the moon,
Glides glimmering o'er my fleece-like floor,
    By the midnight breezes strewn;
And wherever the beat of her unseen feet,
    Which only the angels hear,

May have broken the woof of my tent's thin roof,
    The stars peep behind her and peer;
And I laugh to see them whirl and flee,
    Like a swarm of golden bees,
When I widen the rent in my wind-built tent,
    Till the calm rivers, lakes, and seas,
Like strips of the sky fallen through me on high,
    Are each paved with the moon and these.

I bind the sun's throne with a burning zone,
    And the moon's with a girdle of pearl;
The volcanoes are dim, and the stars reel and swim,
    When the whirlwinds my banner unfurl.
From cape to cape, with a bridge-like shape,
    Over a torrent sea,
Sunbeam-proof, I hang like a roof,
    The mountains its columns be.
The triumphal arch through which I march,
    With hurricane, fire, and snow,
When the powers of the air are chained to my chair,
    Is the million-coloured bow;
The sphere-fire above its soft colours wove,
    While the moist earth was laughing below.

I am the daughter of earth and water,
    And the nursling of the sky;
I pass through the pores of the ocean and shores;
    I change, but I cannot die.

For after the rain when with never a stain,
    The pavilion of heaven is bare,
And the winds and sunbeams with their convex gleams,
    Build up the blue dome of air,
I silently laugh at my own cenotaph,
    And out of the caverns of rain,
Like a child from the womb, like a ghost from the tomb,
    I arise and unbuild it again.

The Aziola

I

"Do you not hear the Aziola cry?
  Methinks she must be nigh,"
    Said Mary, as we sate
In dusk, ere stars were lit, or candles brought;
    And I, who thought
This Aziola was some tedious woman,
    Asked, "Who is Aziola?" How elate
I felt to know that it was nothing human,
  No mockery of myself to fear or hate!
    And Mary saw my soul,
And laugh'd, and said, "Disquiet yourself not,
    'Tis nothing but a little downy owl."

2

Sad Aziola! many an eventide
  Thy music I had heard
By wood and stream, meadow and mountain-side,
And fields and marshes wide,—
  Such as nor voice, nor lute, nor wind, nor bird,
  The soul ever stirr'd;
Unlike, and far sweeter than them all—
Sad Aziola! from that moment, I
  Loved thee, and thy sad cry.

To the Moon

Art thou pale for weariness
Of climbing heaven and gazing on the earth,
Wandering companionless
Among the stars that have a different birth,—
And ever changing, like a joyless eye
That finds no object worth its constancy?

from Evening: Ponte al Mare, Pisa

1

The sun is set; the swallows are asleep;
   The bats are flitting fast in the gray air;
The slow soft toads out of damp corners creep,
   And evening's breath, wandering here and there
Over the quivering surface of the stream,
Wakes not one ripple from its summer dream.

2

There is no dew on the dry grass to-night,
   Nor damp within the shadow of the trees;
The wind is intermitting, dry, and light;
   And in the inconstant motion of the breeze
The dust and straws are driven up and down,
And whirled about the pavement of the town.

. . . . .

4

The chasm in which the sun has sunk is shut
   By darkest barriers of cinereous cloud,
Like mountain over mountain huddled—but
   Growing and moving upwards in a crowd,
And over it a space of watery blue,
Which the keen evening star is shining through.

from Hellas

Ahasuerus.   . . . Earth and ocean,
Space, and the isles of life or light that gem
The sapphire floods of interstellar air,
This firmament pavilioned upon chaos,
With all its cressets of immortal fire,
Whose outwall, bastioned impregnably
Against the escape of boldest thoughts, repels them
As Calpe the Atlantic clouds—this Whole
Of suns, and worlds, and men, and beasts, and flowers,
With all the silent or tempestuous workings
By which they have been, are, or cease to be,
Is but a vision;—all that it inherits
Are motes of a sick eye, bubbles and dreams;
Thought is its cradle and its grave, nor less
The future and the past are idle shadows
Of thought's eternal flight—they have no being;
Nought is but that it feels itself to be.

(lines 769–785)

Music

1

I pant for the music which is divine,
  My heart in its thirst is a dying flower;
Pour forth the sound like enchanted wine,
  Loosen the notes in a silver shower;
Like a herbless plain, for the gentle rain,
I gasp, I faint, till they wake again.

2

Let me drink of the spirit of that sweet sound,
  More, oh more,—I am thirsting yet;
It loosens the serpent which care has bound
  Upon my heart to stifle it;
The dissolving strain, through every vein,
  Passes into my heart and brain.

3

As the scent of a violet withered up,
  Which grew by the brink of a silver lake,
When the hot noon has drained its dewy cup,
  And mist there was none its thirst to slake—
And the violet lay dead while the odour flew
On the wings of the wind o'er the waters blue—

4

As one who drinks from a charmèd cup
   Of foaming, and sparkling, and murmuring wine,
Whom, a mighty Enchantress filling up,
   Invites to love with her kiss divine . . .

from Alastor or the Spirit of Solitude

   . . . Nature's most secret steps
He like her shadow has pursued, where'er
The red volcano overcanopies
Its fields of snow and pinnacles of ice
With burning smoke, or where bitumen lakes
On black bare pointed islets ever beat
With sluggish surge, or where the secret caves
Rugged and dark, winding among the springs
Of fire and poison, inaccessible
To avarice or pride, their starry domes
Of diamond and of gold expand above
Numberless and immeasurable halls,
Frequent with crystal column, and clear shrines
Of pearl, and thrones radiant with chrysolite.
Nor had that scene of ampler majesty
Than gems or gold, the varying roof of heaven
And the green earth lost in his heart its claims

To love and wonder; he would linger long
In lonesome vales, making the wild his home,
Until the doves and squirrels would partake
From his innocuous hand his bloodless food,
Lured by the gentle meaning of his looks,
And the wild antelope, that starts whene'er
The dry leaf rustles in the brake, suspend
Her timid steps to gaze upon a form
More graceful than her own.

(lines 81–106)

The noonday sun
Now shone upon the forest, one vast mass
Of mingling shade, whose brown magnificence
A narrow vale embosoms. There, huge caves,
Scooped in the dark base of their aëry rocks
Mocking its moans, respond and roar for ever.
The meeting boughs and implicated leaves
Wove twilight o'er the Poet's path, as led
By love, or dream, or god, or mightier Death,
He sought in Nature's dearest haunt, some bank,
Her cradle, and his sepulchre. More dark
And dark the shades accumulate. The oak,
Expanding its immense and knotty arms,
Embraces the light beech. The pyramids
Of the tall cedar overarching, frame
Most solemn domes within, and far below,

Like clouds suspended in an emerald sky,
The ash and the acacia floating hang
Tremulous and pale. Like restless serpents, clothed
In rainbow and in fire, the parasites,
Starr'd with ten thousand blossoms, flow around
The grey trunks, and, as gamesome infants' eyes,
With gentle meanings, and most innocent wiles,
Fold their beams round the hearts of those that love,
These twine their tendrils with the wedded boughs
Uniting their close union; the woven leaves
Make net-work of the dark blue light of day,
And the night's noontide clearness, mutable
As shapes in the weird clouds. Soft mossy lawns
Beneath these canopies extend their swells,
Fragrant with perfumed herbs, and eyed with blooms
Minute yet beautiful. One darkest glen
Sends from its woods of musk-rose, twined with jasmine,
A soul-dissolving odour, to invite
To some more lovely mystery. . . .

(lines 420–454)

Fragment: "When Soft Winds and Sunny Skies"

When soft winds and sunny skies
With the green earth harmonize,
And the young and dewy dawn,
Bold as an unhunted fawn,
Up the windless heaven is gone,—
Laugh—for ambushed in the day,—
Clouds and whirlwinds watch their prey.

Fragment: Wine of the Fairies

I am drunk with the honey wine
Of the moon-unfolded eglantine,
Which fairies catch in hyacinth bowls.
The bats, the dormice, and the moles
Sleep in the walls or under the sward
Of the desolate castle yard;
And when 'tis spilt on the summer earth
    Or its fumes arise among the dew,
Their jocund dreams are full of mirth,
      They gibber their joy in sleep; for few
      Of the fairies bear those bowls so new!

The Question

1

I dreamed that, as I wandered by the way,
  Bare Winter suddenly was changed to Spring,
And gentle odours led my steps astray,
  Mixed with a sound of waters murmuring
Along a shelving bank of turf, which lay
  Under a copse, and hardly dared to fling
Its green arms round the bosom of the stream,
But kissed it and then fled, as thou mightest in dream.

2

There grew pied wind-flowers and violets,
  Daisies, those pearled Arcturi of the earth,
The constellated flower that never sets;
  Faint oxslips; tender bluebells, at whose birth
The sod scarce heaved; and that tall flower that wets—
  Like a child, half in tenderness and mirth—
Its mother's face with Heaven's collected tears,
When the low wind, its playmate's voice, it hears.

3

And in the warm hedge grew lush eglantine,
  Green cowbind and the moonlight-coloured may,

And cherry-blossoms, and white cups, whose wine
   Was the bright dew, yet drained not by the day;
And wild roses, and ivy serpentine,
   With its dark buds and leaves, wandering astray;
And flowers azure, black, and streaked with gold,
Fairer than any wakened eyes behold.

4

And nearer to the river's trembling edge
   There grew broad flag-flowers, purple pranked with
      white,
And starry river buds among the sedge,
   And floating water-lilies, broad and bright,
Which lit the oak that overhung the hedge
   With moonlight beams of their own watery light;
And bulrushes, and reeds of such deep green
As soothed the dazzled eye with sober sheen.

5

Methought that of these visionary flowers
   I made a nosegay, bound in such a way
That the same hues, which in their natural bowers
   Were mingled or opposed, the like array
Kept these imprisoned children of the Hours
   Within my hand,—and then, elate and gay,
I hastened to the spot whence I had come,
That I might there present it!—Oh! to whom?

·III·
LOVE
AND
FRIENDSHIP

"Love is the universal thirst for a communion not merely of the senses, but of our whole nature, intellectual, imaginative and sensitive."

—"MANNERS OF THE ANCIENT GREEKS"

from Prometheus Unbound

Asia,   . . . all love is sweet,
Given or returned. Common as light is love,
And its familiar voice wearies not ever.
Like the wide heaven, the all-sustaining air,
It makes the reptile equal to the God:
They who inspire it most are fortunate,
As I am now; but those who feel it most
Are happier still, after long sufferings,
As I shall soon become.

                (Act II, scene 5, lines 39–46)

Love's Philosophy

I

The fountains mingle with the river
    And the rivers with the Ocean,
The winds of Heaven mix for ever
    With a sweet emotion;
Nothing in the world is single;
    All things by a law divine
In one spirit meet and mingle
    Why not I with thine?—

2

See the mountains kiss high Heaven
    And the waves clasp one another;
No sister-flower would be forgiven
    If it disdained its brother;
And the sunlight clasps the earth,
    And the moonbeams kiss the sea:
What is all this sweet work worth
    If thou kiss not me?

3

Follow to the deep wood, sweetest,
Follow to the wild-briar dingle,
Where we seek to intermingle,
And the violet tells no tale
To the odour-scented gale,
For they two have enough to do
Of such work as I and you.

To ———

1

I fear thy kisses, gentle maiden,
    Thou needest not fear mine;
My spirit is too deeply laden
    Ever to burthen thine.

2

I fear thy mien, thy tones, thy motion,
    Thou needest not fear mine;
Innocent is the heart's devotion
    With which I worship thine.

To ———

Music, when soft voices die,
Vibrates in the memory—
Odours, when sweet violets sicken,
Live within the sense they quicken.

Rose leaves, when the rose is dead,
  Are heaped for the belovèd's bed;
And so thy thoughts, when thou art gone,
Love itself shall slumber on.

To ———

1

One word is too often profaned
    For me to profane it,
One feeling too falsely disdained
    For thee to disdain it.
One hope is too like despair
    For prudence to smother,
And Pity from thee more dear
    Than that from another.

2

I can give not what men call love,
    But wilt thou accept not
The worship the heart lifts above
    And the Heavens reject not:
The desire of the moth for the star,
    Of the night for the morrow,
The devotion to something afar
    From the sphere of our sorrow?

With a Guitar: To Jane

Ariel to Miranda:—Take
This slave of music, for the sake
Of him, who is the slave of thee;
And teach it all the harmony
In which thou canst, and only thou,
Make the delighted spirit glow,
Till joy denies itself again,
And, too intense, is turned to pain;
For by permission and command
Of thine own Prince Ferdinand,
Poor Ariel sends this silent token
Of love that never can be spoken;
Your guardian spirit, Ariel, who
From life to life must still pursue
Your happiness,—for thus alone
Can Ariel ever find his own.
From Prospero's enchanted cell,
As the mighty verses tell,
To the throne of Naples he
Lit you o'er the trackless sea,
Flitting on, your prow before,
Like a living meteor.
When you die, the silent Moon,
In her interlunar swoon,
Is not sadder in her cell

Than deserted Ariel;
When you live again on Earth,
Like an unseen Star of birth,
Ariel guides you o'er the sea
Of life from your nativity;
Many changes have been run
Since Ferdinand and you begun
Your course of love, and Ariel still
Has tracked your steps and served your will.
Now, in humbler, happier lot,
This is all remembered not;
And now, alas! the poor sprite is
Imprisoned for some fault of his
In a body like a grave.—
From you, he only dares to crave
For his service and his sorrow,
A smile to-day, a song to-morrow.

The artist who this idol wrought
To echo all harmonious thought,
Felled a tree, while on the steep
The woods were in their winter sleep,
Rocked in that repose divine
On the wind-swept Apennine;
And dreaming, some of autumn past,
And some of spring approaching fast,
And some of April birds and showers,

And some of songs in July bowers,
And all of love,—and so this tree—
O that such our death may be!—
Died in sleep, and felt no pain,
To live in happier form again,
From which, beneath Heaven's fairest star,
The artist wrought this lov'd guitar,
And taught it justly to reply
To all who question skilfully,
In language gentle as thine own;
Whispering in enamoured tone
Sweet oracles of woods and dells
And summer winds in sylvan cells;
For it had learned all harmonies
Of the plains and of the skies,
Of the forests and the mountains,
And the many-voicèd fountains,
The clearest echoes of the hills,
The softest notes of falling rills,
The melodies of birds and bees,
The murmuring of summer seas,
And pattering rain and breathing dew
And airs of evening; and it knew
That seldom-heard mysterious sound,
Which, driven on its diurnal round
As it floats through boundless day,
Our world enkindles on its way—

All this it knows, but will not tell
To those who cannot question well
The spirit that inhabits it:
It talks according to the wit
Of its companions, and no more
Is heard than has been felt before
By those who tempt it to betray
These secrets of an elder day:
But, sweetly as its answers will
Flatter hands of perfect skill,
It keeps its highest, holiest tone
For our belovèd Jane alone.

from Epipsychidion

I never thought before my death to see
Youth's vision thus made perfect. Emily,
I love thee; though the world by no thin name
Will hide that love, from its unvalued shame.
Would we two had been twins of the same mother!
Or, that the name my heart lent to another
Could be a sister's bond for her and thee,
Blending two beams of one eternity!
Yet were one lawful and the other true,
These names, though dear, could paint not, as is due,
How beyond refuge I am thine. Ah me!
I am not thine: I am a part of *thee.*

(lines 42–52)

                      O too late
Belovèd! O too soon adored, by me!
For in the fields of immortality
My spirit should at first have worshipped thine,
A divine presence in a place divine;
Or should have moved beside it on this earth,
A shadow of that substance, from its birth;
But not as now:—I love thee; yes, I feel
That on the fountain of my heart a seal
Is set, to keep its waters pure and bright

For thee, since in those *tears* thou hast delight.
We—are we not formed, as notes of music are,
For one another, though dissimilar;
Such difference without discord, as can make
Those sweetest sounds, in which all spirits shake,
As trembling leaves in a continuous air?

Thy wisdom speaks in me, and bids me dare
Beacon the rocks on which high hearts are wreckt.
I never was attached to that great sect,
Whose doctrine is, that each one should select
Out of the crowd a mistress or a friend,
And all the rest, though fair and wise, commend
To cold oblivion, though it is in the code
Of modern morals, and the beaten road
Which those poor slaves with weary footsteps tread,
Who travel to their home among the dead
By the broad highway of the world, and so
With one chained friend, perhaps a jealous foe,
The dreariest and the longest journey go.

True Love in this differs from gold and clay,
That to divide is not to take away.
Love is like understanding, that grows bright,
Gazing on many truths; 'tis like thy light,
Imagination! which from earth and sky,
And from the depths of human phantasy,

As from a thousand prisms and mirrors, fills
The Universe with glorious beams, and kills
Error, the worm, with many a sun-like arrow
Of its reverberated lightning. Narrow
The heart that loves, the brain that contemplates,
The life that wears, the spirit that creates
One object, and one form, and builds thereby
A sepulchre for its eternity.

(lines 131–173)

Our breath shall intermix, our bosoms bound,
And our veins beat together; and our lips
With other eloquence than words, eclipse
The soul that burns between them, and the wells
Which boil under our being's inmost cells,
The fountains of our deepest life, shall be
Confused in passion's golden purity,
As mountain-springs under the morning Sun.
We shall become the same, we shall be one
Spirit within two frames, oh! wherefore two?
One passion in twin-hearts, which grows and grew,
Till like two meteors of expanding flame,
Those spheres instinct with it become the same,
Touch, mingle, are transfigured; ever still
Burning, yet ever inconsumable:

In one another's substance finding food,
Like flames too pure and light and unimbued
To nourish their bright lives with baser prey,
Which point to Heaven and cannot pass away:
One hope within two wills, one will beneath
Two overshadowing minds, one life, one death,
One Heaven, one Hell, one immortality,
And one annihilation. Woe is me!
The wingèd words on which my soul would pierce
Into the height of love's rare Universe,
Are chains of lead around its flight of fire.—
I pant, I sink, I tremble, I expire!

(lines 565–591)

Good-Night

Good-Night? ah! no; the hour is ill
    Which severs those it should unite;
Let us remain together still,
    Then it will be *good* night.

How can I call the lone night good,
    Though thy sweet wishes wing its flight?
Be it not said, thought, understood—
    Then it will be—*good* night.

To hearts which near each other move
    From evening close to morning light,
The night is good; because, my love,
    They never *say* good-night.

Letter to Maria Gisborne

The spider spreads her webs, whether she be
In poet's tower, cellar, or barn, or tree;
The silk-worm in the dark green mulberry leaves
His winding sheet and cradle ever weaves;
So I, a thing whom moralists call worm,
Sit spinning still round this decaying form,
From the fine threads of rare and subtle thought—
No net of words in garish colours wrought
To catch the idle buzzers of the day—
But a soft cell, where when that fades away,
Memory may clothe in wings my living name
And feed it with the asphodels of fame,
Which in those hearts which must remember me
Grow, making love an immortality.

Whoever should behold me now, I wist,
Would think I were a mighty mechanist,
Bent with sublime Archimedean art
To breathe a soul into the iron heart
Of some machine portentous, or strange gin,
Which by the force of figured spells might win
Its way over the sea, and sport therein;
For round the walls are hung dread engines, such
As Vulcan never wrought for Jove to clutch
Ixion or the Titan:—or the quick

Wit of that man of God, St. Dominic,
To convince Atheist, Turk, or Heretic;
Or those in philanthropic council met,
Who thought to pay some interest for the debt
They owed to Jesus Christ for their salvation,
By giving a faint foretaste of damnation
To Shakespeare, Sidney, Spenser, and the rest
Who made our land an island of the blest.
When lamp-like Spain, who now relumes her fire
On Freedom's hearth, grew dim with Empire:—
With thumbscrews, wheels, with tooth and spike and jag,
Which fishers found under the utmost crag
Of Cornwall and the storm-encompassed isles,
Where to the sky the rude sea rarely smiles
Unless in treacherous wrath, as on the morn
When the exulting elements in scorn,
Satiated with destroyed destruction, lay
Sleeping in beauty on their mangled prey,
As panthers sleep;—and other strange and dread
Magical forms the brick floor overspread,—
Proteus transformed to metal did not make
More figures, or more strange; nor did he take
Such shapes of unintelligible brass,
Or heap himself in such a horrid mass
Of tin and iron not to be understood;
And forms of unimaginable wood,
To puzzle Tubal Cain and all his brood:

Great screws, and cones, and wheels, and groovèd blocks,
The elements of what will stand the shocks
Of wave and wind and time.—Upon the table
More knacks and quips there be than I am able
To catalogize in this verse of mine:—
A pretty bowl of wood—not full of wine,
But quicksilver; that dew which the gnomes drink
When at their subterranean toil they swink,
Pledging the demons of the earthquake, who
Reply to them in lava—cry halloo!
And call out to the cities o'er their head,—
Roofs, towers, and shrines, the dying and the dead,
Crash through the chinks of earth—and then all quaff
Another rouse, and hold their sides and laugh.
This quicksilver no gnome has drunk—within
The walnut bowl it lies, veinèd and thin,
In colour like the wake of light that stains
The Tuscan deep, when from the moist moon rains
The inmost shower of its white fire—the breeze
Is still—blue Heaven smiles over the pale seas,
And in this bowl of quicksilver—for I
Yield to the impulse of an infancy
Outlasting manhood—I have made to float
A rude idealism of a paper boat:—
A hollow screw with cogs—Henry will know
The thing I mean and laugh at me,—if so
He fears not I should do more mischief.—Next

Lie bills and calculations much perplexed,
With steam-boats, frigates, and machinery quaint
Traced over them in blue and yellow paint.
Then comes a range of mathematical
Instruments, for plans nautical and statical;
A heap of rosin, a queer broken glass
With ink in it;—a china cup that was
What it will never be again, I think,—
A thing from which sweet lips were wont to drink
The liquor doctors rail at—and which I
Will quaff in spite of them—and when we die
We'll toss up who died first of drinking tea,
And cry out,—"Heads or tails?" where'er we be.
Near that a dusty paint-box, some odd hooks,
A half-burnt match, an ivory block, three books,
Where conic sections, spherics, logarithms,
To great Laplace, from Saunderson and Sims,
Lie heaped in their harmonious disarray
Of figure,—disentangle them who may.
Baron de Tott's Memoirs beside them lie,
And some odd volumes of old chemistry.
Near those a most inexplicable thing,
With lead in the middle—I'm conjecturing
How to make Henry understand; but no—
I'll leave, as Spenser says, with many mo,
This secret in the pregnant womb of time,
Too vast a matter for so weak a rhyme.

And here like some weird Archimage sit I,
Plotting dark spells, and devilish enginery,
The self-impelling steam-wheels of the mind
Which pump up oaths from clergymen, and grind
The gentle spirit of our meek reviews
Into a powdery foam of salt abuse,
Ruffling the ocean of their self-content;—
I sit—and smile or sigh as is my bent,
But not for them—Libeccio rushes round
With an inconstant and an idle sound,
I heed him more than them—the thunder-smoke
Is gathering on the mountains, like a cloak
Folded athwart their shoulders broad and bare;
The ripe corn under the undulating air
Undulates like an ocean;—and the vines
Are trembling wide in all their trellised lines;—
The murmur of the awakening sea doth fill
The empty pauses of the blast;—the hill
Looks hoary through the white electric rain,
And from the glens beyond, in sullen strain
The interrupted thunder howls; above
One chasm of heaven smiles, like the eye of love
On the unquiet world;—while such things are,
How could one worth your friendship heed the war
Of worms? The shriek of the world's carrion jays,
Their censure, or their wonder, or their praise?

You are not here! the quaint witch Memory sees
In vacant chairs your absent images,
And points where once you sat, and now should be
But are not.—I demand if ever we
Shall meet as then we met;—and she replies,
Veiling in awe her second-sighted eyes;
"I know the past alone—but summon home
My sister Hope,—she speaks of all to come."
But I, an old diviner, who knew well
Every false verse of that sweet oracle,
Turned to the sad enchantress once again,
And sought a respite from my gentle pain,
In citing every passage o'er and o'er
Of our communion—how on the sea-shore
We watched the ocean and the sky together,
Under the roof of blue Italian weather;
How I ran home through last year's thunder-storm,
And felt the transverse lightning linger warm
Upon my cheek—and how we often made
Feasts for each other, where good will outweighed
The frugal luxury of our country cheer,
As well it might, were it less firm and clear
Than ours must ever be;—and how we spun
A shroud of talk to hide us from the sun
Of this familiar life, which seems to be
But is not,—or is but quaint mockery

Of all we would believe, and sadly blame
The jarring and inexplicable frame
Of this wrong world:—and then anatomize
The purposes and thoughts of men whose eyes
Were closed in distant years;—or widely guess
The issue of the earth's great business,
When we shall be as we no longer are—
Like babbling gossips safe, who hear the war
Of winds, and sigh, but tremble not; or how
You listened to some interrupted flow
Of visionary rhyme,—in joy and pain
Struck from the inmost fountains of my brain,
With little skill perhaps;—or how we sought
Those deepest wells of passion or of thought
Wrought by wise poets in the waste of years,
Staining their sacred waters with our tears;
Quenching a thirst ever to be renewed!
Or how I, wisest lady! then endued
The language of a land which now is free,
And winged with thoughts of truth and majesty,
Flits round the tyrant's sceptre like a cloud,
And bursts the peopled prisons, and cries aloud,
"My name is Legion!"—that majestic tongue
Which Calderon over the desert flung
Of ages and of nations; and which found
An echo in our hearts, and with the sound
Startled oblivion;—thou wert then to me

As is a nurse—when inarticulately
A child would talk as its grown parents do.
If living winds the rapid clouds pursue,
If hawks chase doves through the aethereal way,
Huntsmen the innocent deer, and beasts their prey,
Why should not we rouse with the spirit's blast
Out of the forest of the pathless past
These recollected pleasures?

            You are now
In London, that great sea, whose ebb and flow
At once is deaf and loud, and on the shore
Vomits its wrecks, and still howls on for more.
Yet in its depth what treasures! You will see
That which was Godwin,—greater none than he;
Though fallen—and fallen on evil times—to stand
Among the spirits of our age and land,
Before the dread tribunal of *to come*
The foremost,—while Rebuke cowers pale and dumb.
You will see Coleridge—he who sits obscure
In the exceeding lustre and the pure
Intense irradiation of a mind,
Which, with its own internal lightning blind,
Flags wearily through darkness and despair—
A cloud-encircled meteor of the air,
A hooded eagle among blinking owls.

You will see Hunt—one of those happy souls
Which are the salt of the earth, and without whom
This world would smell like what it is—a tomb;
Who is, what others seem;—his room no doubt
Is still adorned with many a cast from Shout,
With graceful flowers tastefully placed about;
And coronals of bay from ribbons hung;
And brighter wreaths in neat disorder flung;
The gifts of the most learn'd among some dozens
Of female friends, sisters-in-law, and cousins.
And there is he with his eternal puns,
Which beat the dullest brain for smiles, like duns
Thundering for money at a poet's door;
Alas! it is no use to say, "I'm poor!"
Or oft in graver mood, when he will look
Things wiser than were ever read in book,
Except in Shakespeare's wisest tenderness.
You will see Hogg, and I cannot express
His virtues, though I know that they are great,
Because he locks, then barricades the gate
Within which they inhabit;—of his wit,
And wisdom, you'll cry out when you are bit.
He is a pearl within an oyster-shell,
One of the richest of the deep. And there
Is English Peacock, with his mountain Fair
Turned into a Flamingo,—that shy bird

That gleams i' the Indian air—have you not heard
When a man marries, dies, or turns Hindoo,
His best friends hear no more of him? But you
Will see him, and will like him too, I hope,
With the milk-white Snowdonian Antelope
Matched with this cameleopard; his fine wit
Makes such a wound, the knife is lost in it;
A strain too learnèd for a shallow age,
Too wise for selfish bigots;—let his page,
Which charms the chosen spirits of the time,
Fold itself up for the serener clime
Of years to come, and find its recompense
In that just expectation. Wit and sense,
Virtue and human knowledge, all that might
Make this dull world a business of delight,
Are all combined in Horace Smith.—And these,
With some exceptions, which I need not teaze
Your patience by descanting on, are all
You and I know in London.

              I recall
My thoughts, and bid you look upon the night.
As water does a sponge, so the moonlight
Fills the void, hollow, universal air.
What see you?—Unpavilioned heaven is fair,
Whether the moon, into her chamber gone,

Leaves midnight to the golden stars, or wan
Climbs with diminished beams the azure steep;
Or whether clouds sail o'er the inverse deep,
Piloted by the many-wandering blast,
And the rare stars rush through them, dim and fast.
All this is beautiful in every land.
But what see you beside? A shabby stand
Of Hackney-coaches—a brick house or wall
Fencing some lonely court, white with the scrawl
Of our unhappy politics;—or worse—
A wretched woman reeling by, whose curse
Mixed with the watchman's, partner of her trade,
You must accept in place of serenade—
Or yellow-haired Pollonia murmuring
To Henry, some unutterable thing.
I see a chaos of green leaves and fruit
Built round dark caverns, even to the root
Of the living stems that feed them; in whose bowers
There sleep in their dark dew the folded flowers;
Beyond, the surface of the unsickled corn
Trembles not in the slumbering air, and borne
In circles quaint, and ever-changing dance,
Like wingèd stars the fire-flies flash and glance
Pale in the open moonshine, but each one
Under the dark trees seems a little sun,
A meteor tamed; a fixed star gone astray
From the silver regions of the milky way.

Afar the Contadino's song is heard,
Rude, but made sweet by distance;—and a bird
Which cannot be the nightingale, and yet
I know none else that sings so sweet as it
At this late hour;—and then all is still.—
Now, Italy or London, which you will!

Next winter you must pass with me: I'll have
My house by that time turned into a grave
Of dead despondence and low-thoughted care,
And all the dreams which our tormentors are.
Oh! that Hunt, Hogg, Peacock, and Smith were there,
With every thing belonging to them fair!—
We will have books; Spanish, Italian, Greek,
And ask one week to make another week
As like his father, as I'm unlike mine,
Which is not his fault, as you may divine.
Though we eat little flesh and drink no wine.
Yet let's be merry: we'll have tea and toast;
Custards for supper, and an endless host
Of syllabubs and jellies and mince-pies,
And other such lady-like luxuries,—
Feasting on which we will philosophize!
And we'll have fires out of the Grand Duke's wood,
To thaw the six weeks' winter in our blood.
And then we'll talk;—what shall we talk about?
Oh! there are themes enough for many a bout

Of thought-entangled descant;—as to nerves—
With cones and parallelograms and curves
I've sworn to strangle them if once they dare
To bother me—when you are with me there.
And they shall never more sip laudanum
From Helicon or Himeros;—well, come,
And in despite of God and of the devil,
We'll make our friendly philosophic revel
Outlast the leafless time; till buds and flowers
Warn the obscure inevitable hours
Sweet meeting by sad parting to renew;—
"To-morrow to fresh woods and pastures new."

To Constantia, Singing

1

Thus to be lost and thus to sink and die,
    Perchance were death indeed!—Constantia, turn!
In thy dark eyes a power like light doth lie,
    Even though the sounds which were thy voice, which
        burn
Between thy lips, are laid to sleep;
    Within thy breath, and on thy hair, like odour, it is
        yet,
And from thy touch like fire doth leap.
    Even while I write, my burning cheeks are wet,
    Alas, that the torn heart can bleed, but not forget!

2

A breathless awe, like the swift change
    Unseen, but felt in youthful slumbers,
Wild, sweet, but uncommunicably strange,
    Thou breathest now in fast ascending numbers.
The cope of heaven seems rent and cloven
    By the enchantment of thy strain,
And on my shoulders wings are woven,

To follow its sublime career
Beyond the mighty moons that wane
　　Upon the verge of Nature's utmost sphere,
　　Till the world's shadowy walls are past and disappear.

3

Her voice is hovering o'er my soul—it lingers
　　O'ershadowing it with soft and lulling wings,
The blood and life within those snowy fingers
　　Teach witchcraft to the instrumental strings.
My brain is wild, my breath comes quick—
　　The blood is listening in my frame,
And thronging shadows, fast and thick,
　　Fall on my overflowing eyes;
My heart is quivering like a flame;
　　As morning dew, that in the sunbeam dies,
　　I am dissolved in these consuming ecstasies.

4

I have no life, Constantia, now, but thee,
　　Whilst, like the world-surrounding air, thy song
Flows on, and fills all things with melody.—
　　Now is thy voice a tempest swift and strong,
On which, like one in trance upborne,

Secure o'er rocks and waves I sweep,
Rejoicing like a cloud of morn.
Now 'tis the breath of summer night,
Which when the starry waters sleep,
Round western isles, with incense-blossoms bright
Lingering, suspends my soul in its voluptuous flight.

·IV·
LOSS
AND
LAMENTATION

"Men do well to mourn for the dead: it proves that we love something beside ourselves."

—"THE DEATH OF PRINCESS CHARLOTTE"

A Lament

O world! O life! O time!
On whose last steps I climb,
   Trembling at that where I had stood before;
When will return the glory of your prime?
     No more—oh, never more!

Out of the day and night
A joy has taken flight;
   Fresh spring, and summer, and winter hoar,
Move my faint heart with grief, but with delight
     No more—oh, never more!

Mutability

1

The flower that smiles to-day
    To-morrow dies;
All that we wish to stay
    Tempts and then flies.
What is this world's delight?
Lightning that mocks the night,
    Brief even as bright.

2

Virtue, how frail it is!
    Friendship how rare!
Love, how it sells poor bliss
    For proud despair!
But we, though soon they fall,
Survive their joy, and all
    Which ours we call.

3

Whilst skies are blue and bright,
    Whilst flowers are gay,
Whilst eyes that change ere night
    Make glad the day;

Whilst yet the calm hours creep,
Dream thou—and from thy sleep
Then wake to weep.

To ———

When passion's trance is overpast,
If tenderness and truth could last,
Or live, whilst all wild feelings keep
Some mortal slumber, dark and deep,
I should not weep, I should not weep!

It were enough to feel, to see
Thy soft eyes gazing tenderly,
And dream the rest—and burn and be
The secret food of fires unseen,
Couldst thou but be as thou hast been.

After the slumber of the year
The woodland violets reappear;
All things revive in field or grove,
And sky and sea, but two, which move
And form all others, life and love.

To Wordsworth

Poet of Nature, thou hast wept to know
That things depart which never may return:
Childhood and youth, friendship and love's first glow,
Have fled like sweet dreams, leaving thee to mourn.
These common woes I feel. One loss is mine
Which thou too feel'st, yet I alone deplore.
Thou wert as a lone star, whose light did shine
On some frail bark in winter's midnight roar:
Thou hast like to a rock-built refuge stood
Above the blind and battling multitude:
In honoured poverty thy voice did weave
Songs consecrate to truth and liberty,—
Deserting these, thou leavest me to grieve,
Thus having been, that thou shouldst cease to be.

To Night

1

Swiftly walk o'er the western wave,
     Spirit of Night!
Out of the misty eastern cave
Where, all the long and lone daylight,
Thou wovest dreams of joy and fear,
Which make thee terrible and dear,—
     Swift be thy flight!

2

Wrap thy form in a mantle gray,
     Star-inwrought!
Blind with thine hair the eyes of Day,
Kiss her until she be wearied out,
Then wander o'er city, and sea, and land,
Touching all with thine opiate wand—
     Come, long-sought!

3

When I arose and saw the dawn,
     I sighed for thee;
When light rode high, and the dew was gone,
And noon lay heavy on flower and tree,
And the weary Day turned to his rest,
Lingering like an unloved guest,
     I sighed for thee.

4

Thy brother Death came, and cried,
     Wouldst thou me?
Thy sweet child Sleep, the filmy-eyed,
Murmured like a noon-tide bee,
Shall I nestle near thy side?
Wouldst thou me?—And I replied,
     No, . . . not thee!

5

Death will come when thou art dead,
     Soon, too soon—
Sleep will come when thou art fled;
Of neither would I ask the boon
I ask of thee, belovèd Night—
Swift be thine approaching flight,
     Come soon, soon!

The World's Wanderers

1

Tell me, thou Star, whose wings of light
Speed thee in thy fiery flight,
In what cavern of the night
    Will thy pinions close now?

2

Tell me, Moon, thou pale and gray
Pilgrim of Heaven's homeless way,
In what depth of night or day
    Seekest thou repose now?

3

Weary Wind, who wanderest
Like the world's rejected guest,
Hast thou still some secret nest
    On the tree or billow?

Time Long Past

1

Like the ghost of a dear friend dead
    Is Time long past.
A tone which is now forever fled,
A hope which is now forever past,
A love so sweet it could not last,
    Was Time long past.

2

There were sweet dreams in the night
    Of Time long past:
And, was it sadness or delight,
Each day a shadow onward cast
Which made us wish it yet might last—
    That Time long past.

3

There is regret, almost remorse,
    For Time long past.
'Tis like a child's belovèd corse
A father watches, till at last
Beauty is like remembrance, cast
    From Time long past.

Lines to a Reviewer

Alas, good friend, what profit can you see
In hating such a hateless thing as me?
There is no sport in hate where all the rage
Is on one side: in vain would you assuage
Your frowns upon an unresisting smile,
In which not even contempt lurks to beguile
Your heart, by some fain sympathy of hate.
Oh, conquer what you cannot satiate!
For to your passion I am far more coy
Than ever yet was coldest maid or boy
In winter noon. Of your antipathy
If I am the Narcissus, you are free
To pine into a sound with hating me.

Lines: "When the Lamp Is Shattered"

1

When the lamp is shattered,
The light in the dust lies dead—
When the cloud is scattered,
The rainbow's glory is shed.
When the lute is broken,
Sweet tones are remembered not;
When the lips have spoken,
Loved accents are soon forgot.

2

As music and splendour
Survive not the lamp and the lute,
The heart's echoes render
No song when the spirit is mute:—
No song but sad dirges,
Like the wind through a ruined cell,
Or the mournful surges
That ring the dead seaman's knell.

3

When hearts have once mingled,
Love first leaves the well-built nest;

The weak one is singled
To endure what it once possessed.
O Love! who bewailest
The frailty of all things here,
Why choose you the frailest
For your cradle, your home, and your bier?

4

Its passions will rock thee
As the storms rock the ravens on high;
Bright reason will mock thee,
Like the sun from a wintry sky.
From thy nest every rafter
Will rot, and thine eagle home
Leave thee naked to laughter,
When leaves fall and cold winds come.

To the Lord Chancellor

[*This was Lord Eldon, who had declared Shelley unfit to have custody of his two children by his first wife.*]

1

Thy country's curse is on thee, darkest crest
  Of that foul, knotted, many-headed worm
Which rends our Mother's bosom—Priestly Pest!
  Masked Resurrection of a buried Form!

2

Thy country's curse is on thee! Justice sold,
  Truth trampled, Nature's landmarks overthrown,
And heaps of fraud-accumulated gold,
  Plead, loud as thunder, at Destruction's throne.

3

And whilst that slow sure Angel, which aye stands
  Watching the beck of Mutability,
Delays to execute her high commands,
  And, though a nation weeps, spares thine and thee.

4

Oh, let a father's curse be on thy soul,
  And let a daughter's hope be on thy tomb,
And both on thy gray head, a leaden cowl
  To weigh thee down to thine approaching doom!

5

I curse thee by a parent's outraged love,
  By hopes long cherished and too lately lost,
By gentle feelings thou couldst never prove,
  By griefs which thy stern nature never crossed;

6

By those infantine smiles of happy light,
  Which were a fire within a stranger's hearth,
Quenched even when kindled, in untimely night
  Hiding the promise of a lovely birth:

7

By those unpractised accents of young speech,
  Which he who is a father thought to frame
To gentlest lore, such as the wisest teach—
  Thou strike the lyre of mind!—oh, grief and shame!

8

By all the happy see in children's growth—
    That undeveloped flower of budding years—
Sweetness and sadness interwoven both,
    Source of the sweetest hopes and saddest fears—

9

By all the days, under an hireling's care,
    Of dull constraint and bitter heaviness,—
O wretched ye if ever any were,—
    Sadder than orphans, yet not fatherless!

10

By the false cant which on their innocent lips
    Must hang like poison on an opening bloom,
By the dark creeds which cover with eclipse
    Their pathway from the cradle to the tomb—

11

By thy most impious Hell, and all its terrors;
    By all the grief, the madness, and the guilt
Of thine impostures, which must be their error—
    That sand on which thy crumbling power is built—

12

By thy complicity with lust and hate—
   Thy thirst for tears—thy hunger after gold—
The ready frauds which ever on thee wait—
   The servile arts in which thou hast grown old—

13

By thy most killing sneer, and by thy smile—
   By all the snares and arts of thy black den,
And—for thou canst outweep the crocodile—
   By thy false tears—those millstones braining men—

14

By all the hate which checks a father's love—
   By all the scorn which kills a father's care—
By those most impious hands which dared remove
   Nature's high bounds—by thee—and by despair—

15

Yes, the despair which bids a father groan,
   And cry, "My children are no longer mine—
The blood within those veins may be mine own,
   But—Tyrant—their polluted souls are thine;"—

16

I curse thee—though I hate thee not.—O slave!
   If thou couldst quench the earth-consuming Hell
Of which thou art a daemon, on thy grave
   This curse should be a blessing. Fare thee well!

To William Shelley

(With what truth I may say—
Roma! Roma! Roma!
Non è più come era prima!)

1

My lost William, thou in whom
   Some bright spirit lived, and did
That decaying robe consume
   Which its lustre faintly hid,—
Here its ashes find a tomb,—
   But beneath this pyramid
Thou art not—if a thing divine
Like thee can die—thy funeral shrine
Is thy Mother's grief and mine.

2

Where art thou, my gentle child?
   Let me think thy spirit feeds,
With its life intense and mild,
   The love of living leaves and weeds.
Among these tombs and ruins wild
   Let me think that thro' low seeds
Of sweet flowers and sunny grass,
Into their hues and scents may pass,
A portion——

Stanzas

Written in Dejection, near Naples

The sun is warm, the sky is clear,
   The waves are dancing fast and bright,
Blue isles and snowy mountains wear
   The purple noon's transparent might:
   The breath of the moist earth is light,
Around its unexpanded buds;
   Like many a voice of one delight,
The winds, the birds, the ocean floods,
The City's voice itself, is soft like Solitude's.

I see the Deep's untrampled floor
　　With green and purple seaweeds strown;
I see the waves upon the shore,
　　Like light dissolved in star-showers, thrown:
　　I sit upon the sands alone,—
The lightning of the noon-tide ocean
　　Is flashing round me, and a tone
Arises from its measured motion,
How sweet! did any heart now share in my emotion.

Alas! I have nor hope nor health,
　　Nor peace within nor calm around,
Nor that content surpassing wealth
　　The sage in meditation found,
　　And walked with inward glory crowned—
Nor fame, nor power, nor love, nor leisure.
　　Others I see whom these surround—
Smiling they live, and call life pleasure;
To me that cup has been dealt in another measure.

Yet now despair itself is mild,
　　Even as the winds and waters are;
I could lie down like a tired child,
　　And weep away the life of care
　　Which I have borne, and yet must bear,
Till death like sleep steal on me,

And I might feel in the warm air
My cheek grow cold, and hear the sea
Breathe o'er my dying brain its last monotony.

Some might lament that I were cold,
    As I, when this sweet day is gone,
Which my lost heart, too soon grown old,
    Insults with this untimely moan;
    They might lament—for I am one
Whom men love not,—and yet regret,
    Unlike this day, which, when the sun
    Shall on its stainless glory set,
Will linger, though enjoyed, like joy in memory yet.

from Adonais

AN ELEGY ON THE DEATH OF JOHN KEATS,
AUTHOR OF ENDYMION, HYPERION, ETC.

I

I weep for Adonais—he is dead!
Oh, weep for Adonais! though our tears
Thaw not the frost which binds so dear a head!
And thou, sad Hour, selected from all years
To mourn our loss, rouse thy obscure compeers,
And teach them thine own sorrow, say: "With me
Died Adonais; till the Future dares
Forget the Past, his fate and fame shall be
An echo and a light unto eternity!"

.   .   .   .   .

7

To that high Capital, where kingly Death
Keeps his pale court in beauty and decay,
He came; and bought, with price of purest breath,
A grave among the eternal.—Come away!
Haste, while the vault of blue Italian day
Is yet his fitting charnel-roof! while still
He lies, as if in dewy sleep he lay;
Awake him not! surely he takes his fill
Of deep and liquid rest, forgetful of all ill.

8

He will awake no more, oh, never more!—
Within the twilight chamber spreads apace,
The shadow of white Death, and at the door
Invisible Corruption waits to trace
His extreme way to her dim dwelling-place;
The eternal Hunger sits, but pity and awe
Soothe her pale rage, nor dares she to deface
So fair a prey, till darkness, and the law
Of change, shall o'er his sleep the mortal curtain draw.

9

Oh, weep for Adonais!—The quick Dreams,
The passion-wingèd Ministers of thought,
Who were his flocks, whom near the living streams
Of his young spirit he fed, and whom he taught
The love which was its music, wander not,—
Wander no more, from kindling brain to brain,
But droop there, whence they sprung; and mourn their
   lot
Round the cold heart, where, after their sweet pain,
They ne'er will gather strength, or find a home again.

·   ·   ·   ·   ·

18

Ah woe is me! Winter is come and gone,
But grief returns with the revolving year;
The airs and streams renew their joyous tone;
The ants, the bees, the swallows reappear;
Fresh leaves and flowers deck the dead Seasons' bier;
The amorous birds now pair in every brake,
And build their mossy homes in field and brere;
And the green lizard, and the golden snake,
Like unimprisoned flames, out of their trance awake.

. . . . .

30

. . . the mountain shepherds came
Their garlands sere, their magic mantles rent;
The Pilgrim of Eternity, whose fame
Over his living head like Heaven is bent,
An early but enduring monument,
Came, veiling all the lightnings of his song
In sorrow; from her wilds Ierne sent
The sweetest lyrist of her saddest wrong,
And love taught grief to fall like music from his tongue.

31

Midst others of less note, came one frail Form,
A phantom among men; companionless

As the last cloud of an expiring storm,
Whose thunder is its knell; he, as I guess,
Had gazed on Nature's naked loveliness,
Actaeon-like, and now he fled astray
With feeble steps o'er the world's wilderness,
And his own thoughts, along that rugged way,
Pursued, like raging hounds, their father and their prey.

32

A pardlike Spirit beautiful and swift—
A Love in desolation masked;—a Power
Girt round with weakness;—it can scarce uplift
The weight of the superincumbent hour;
It is a dying lamp, a falling shower,
A breaking billow;—even whilst we speak
Is it not broken? On the withering flower
The killing sun smiles brightly: on a cheek
The life can burn in blood, even while the heart may
break.

33

His head was bound with pansies overblown,
And faded violets, white, and pied, and blue;
And a light spear topped with a cypress cone,
Round whose rude shaft dark ivy-tresses grew

Yet dripping with the forest's noon-day dew,
Vibrated, as the ever-beating heart
Shook the weak hand that grasped it; of that crew
He came the last, neglected and apart;
A herd-abandoned deer, struck by the hunter's dart.

· · · · ·

38

Nor let us weep that our delight is fled
Far from these carrion kites that scream below;
He wakes or sleeps with the enduring dead;
Thou canst not soar where he is sitting now.—
Dust to the dust! but the pure spirit shall flow
Back to the burning fountain whence it came,
A portion of the Eternal, which must glow
Through time and change, unquenchably the same,
Whilst thy cold embers choke the sordid hearth of shame.

39

Peace, peace! he is not dead, he doth not sleep—
He hath awakened from the dream of life—
'Tis we, who lost in stormy visions, keep
With phantoms an unprofitable strife,
And in mad trance strike with our spirit's knife
Invulnerable nothings—*We* decay
Like corpses in a charnel; fear and grief

Convulse us and consume us day by day,
And cold hopes swarm like worms within our living clay.

40

He has outsoared the shadow of our night;
Envy and calumny and hate and pain,
And that unrest which men miscall delight,
Can touch him not and torture not again;
From the contagion of the world's slow stain
He is secure, and now can never mourn
A heart grown cold, a head grown grey in vain;
Nor, when the spirit's self has ceased to burn,
With sparkless ashes load an unlamented urn.

41

He lives, he wakes—'tis Death is dead, not he;
Mourn not for Adonais.—Thou young Dawn,
Turn all thy dew to splendour, for from thee
The spirit thou lamentest is not gone;
Ye caverns and ye forests, cease to moan!
Cease ye faint flowers and fountains, and thou Air,
Which like a mourning veil thy scarf hadst thrown
O'er the abandoned earth, now leave it bare
Even to the joyous stars which smile on its despair!

42

He is made one with Nature: there is heard
His voice in all her music, from the moan
Of thunder, to the song of night's sweet bird;
He is a presence to be felt and known
In darkness and in light, from herb and stone,
Spreading itself where'er that Power may move
Which has withdrawn his being to its own;
Which wields the world with never wearied love,
Sustains it from beneath, and kindles it above.

43

He is a portion of the loveliness
Which once he made more lovely: he doth bear
His part, while the one Spirit's plastic stress
Sweeps through the dull dense world, compelling there
All new successions to the forms they wear;
Torturing th' unwilling dross that checks its flight
To its own likeness, as each mass may bear;
And bursting in its beauty and its might
From trees and beasts and men into the Heaven's light.

. . . . .

52

The One remains, the many change and pass;
Heaven's light forever shines, Earth's shadows fly;
Life, like a dome of many-coloured glass,

Stains the white radiance of Eternity,
Until Death tramples it to fragments.—Die,
If thou wouldst be with that which thou dost seek!
Follow where all is fled!—Rome's azure sky,
Flowers, ruins, statues, music, words, are weak
The glory they transfuse with fitting truth to speak.

53

Why linger, why turn back, why shrink, my Heart?
Thy hopes are gone before: from all things here
They have departed; thou shouldst now depart!
A light is past from the revolving year,
And man, and woman; and what still is dear
Attracts to crush, repels to make thee wither.
The soft sky smiles,—the low wind whispers near:
'Tis Adonais calls! oh, hasten thither,
No more let life divide what Death can join together.

54

That Light whose smile kindles the Universe,
That Beauty in which all things work and move,
That Benediction which the eclipsing Curse
Of birth can quench not, that sustaining Love
Which through the web of being blindly wove
By man and beast and earth and air and sea,

Burns bright or dim, as each are mirrors of
    The fire for which all thirst; now beams on me,
Consuming the last clouds of cold mortality.

55

The breath whose might I have invoked in song
Descends on me; my spirit's bark is driven,
Far from the shore, far from the trembling throng
Whose sails were never to the tempest given;
The massy earth and sphered skies are riven!
I am borne darkly, fearfully, afar;
    Whilst burning through the inmost veil of Heaven,
    The soul of Adonais, like a star,
Beacons from the abode where the Eternal are.

A Dirge

Rough wind, that moanest loud
   Grief too sad for song;
Wild wind, when sullen cloud
   Knells all the night long;
Sad storm, whose tears are vain,
Bare woods, whose branches strain,
Deep caves and dreary main,—
   Wail, for the world's wrong!

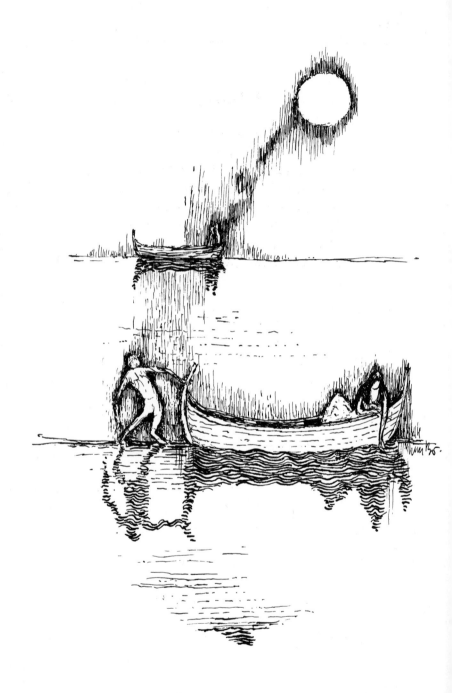

·V·

THE

IMAGINATIVE

IDEAL

"Yet every heart contains perfection's germ."

—QUEEN MAB

from Prometheus Unbound

Third Spirit

I sate beside a sage's bed,
And the lamp was burning red
Near the book where he had fed,
When a Dream with plumes of flame,
To his pillow hovering came,
And I knew it was the same
Which had kindled long ago
Pity, eloquence, and woe;
And the world awhile below
Wore the shade, its lustre made.
It has borne me here as fleet
As Desire's lightning feet:
I must ride it back ere morrow,
Or the sage will wake in sorrow.

Fourth Spirit

On a poet's lip I slept
Dreaming like a love-adept
In the sound his breathing kept;
Nor seeks nor finds he mortal blisses,
But feeds on the aërial kisses
Of shapes that haunt thought's wildernesses.
He will watch from dawn to gloom
The lake-reflected sun illume

The yellow bees in the ivy-bloom,
Nor heed nor see, what things they be;
But from these create he can
Forms more real than living man,
Nurslings of immortality!
One of these awakened me,
And I sped to succour thee.

(Act I, scene 1, lines 723–750)

Hymn to Intellectual Beauty

I

The awful shadow of some unseen Power
  Floats tho' unseen among us; visiting
  This various world with as inconstant wing
As summer winds that creep from flower to flower;
Like moonbeams that behind some piny mountain
    shower,
    It visits with inconstant glance
    Each human heart and countenance;
Like hues and harmonies of evening,
    Like clouds in starlight widely spread,
    Like memory of music fled,
    Like aught that for its grace may be
Dear, and yet dearer for its mystery.

2

Spirit of BEAUTY, that dost consecrate
  With thine own hues all thou dost shine upon
  Of human thought or form, where art thou gone?
Why dost thou pass away and leave our state,
This dim vast vale of tears, vacant and desolate?
    Ask why the sunlight not for ever
    Weaves rainbows o'er yon mountain river,
Why aught should fail and fade that once is shown;
    Why fear and dream and death and birth
    Cast on the daylight of this earth
    Such gloom, why man has such a scope
For love and hate, despondency and hope?

3

No voice from some sublimer world hath ever
  To sage or poet these responses given:
  Therefore the names of Demon, Ghost, and Heaven,
Remain the records of their vain endeavour:
Frail spells, whose uttered charm might not avail to
    sever,
    From all we hear and all we see,
    Doubt, chance, and mutability.
Thy light alone, like mist o'er mountains driven,
    Or music by the night wind sent
    Thro' strings of some still instrument,

Or moonlight on a midnight stream,
Gives grace and truth to life's unquiet dream.

4

Love, Hope, and Self-esteem, like clouds, depart
   And come, for some uncertain moments lent.
   Man were immortal and omnipotent,
Didst thou, unknown and awful as thou art,
Keep with thy glorious train firm state within his heart.
     Thou messenger of sympathies
     That wax and wane in lovers' eyes;
Thou, that to human thought art nourishment,
    Like darkness to a dying flame!
    Depart not as thy shadow came:
    Depart not, lest the grave should be,
Like life and fear, a dark reality.

5

While yet a boy I sought for ghosts, and sped
   Thro' many a listening chamber, cave and ruin,
   And starlight wood, with fearful steps pursuing
Hopes of high talk with the departed dead.
I called on poisonous names with which our youth is fed:
    I was not heard: I saw them not:
    When musing deeply on the lot

Of life, at that sweet time when winds are wooing
    All vital things that wake to bring
    News of birds and blossoming,
    Sudden, thy shadow fell on me;
I shrieked, and clasped my hands in ecstasy!

6

I vowed that I would dedicate my powers
    To thee and thine: have I not kept the vow?
    With beating heart and streaming eyes, even now
I call the phantoms of a thousand hours
Each from his voiceless grave: they have in visioned
    bowers
    Of studious zeal or love's delight
    Outwatched with me the envious night:
They know that never joy illumed my brow,
    Unlinked with hope that thou wouldst free
    This world from its dark slavery,
    That thou, O awful LOVELINESS,
Wouldst give whate'er these words cannot express.

7

The day becomes more solemn and serene
   When noon is past: there is a harmony
   In autumn, and a lustre in its sky,
Which thro' the summer is not heard or seen,
As if it could not be, as if it had not been!
     Thus let thy power, which like the truth
     Of nature on my passive youth
Descended, to my onward life supply
   Its calm, to one who worships thee,
   And every form containing thee,
   Whom, SPIRIT fair, thy spells did bind
To fear himself, and love all human kind.

from Lines Written Among the
Euganean Hills
October, 1818

Other flowering isles must be
In the sea of life and agony:
Other spirits float and flee
O'er that gulf: even now, perhaps,
On some rock the wild wave wraps,
With folded wings they waiting sit
For my bark, to pilot it
To some calm and blooming cove,
Where for me, and those I love,
May a windless bower be built,
Far from passion, pain, and guilt,
In a dell 'mid lawny hills,
Which the wild sea-murmur fills,
And soft sunshine, and the sound
Of old forests echoing round,
And the light and smell divine
Of all flowers that breathe and shine:
We may live so happy there,
That the spirits of the air,
Envying us, may even entice
To our healing paradise
The polluting multitude;

But their rage would be subdued
By that clime divine and calm,
And the winds whose wings rain balm
On the uplifted soul, and leaves
Under which the bright sea heaves:
While each breathless interval
In their whisperings musical
The inspired soul supplies
With its own deep melodies,
And the love which heals all strife
Circling, like the breath of life,
All things in that sweet abode
With its own mild brotherhood:
They, not it, would change; and soon
Every sprite beneath the moon
Would repent its envy vain,
And the earth grow young again.

(lines 335–373)

To a Skylark

1

Hail to thee, blithe Spirit!
  Bird thou never wert,
That from Heaven, or near it,
  Pourest thy full heart
In profuse strains of unpremeditated art.

2

Higher still and higher
  From the earth thou springest
Like a cloud of fire;
  The blue deep thou wingest,
And singing still dost soar, and soaring ever singest.

3

In the golden lightning
  Of the sunken Sun,
O'er which clouds are brightning,
  Thou dost float and run;
Like an unbodied joy whose race is just begun.

4

The pale purple even
  Melts around thy flight;
Like a star of Heaven,
  In the broad day-light
Thou art unseen, but yet I hear thy shrill delight.

5

Keen as are the arrows
Of that silver sphere,
Whose intense lamp narrows
In the white dawn clear,
Until we hardly see, we feel that it is there.

6

All the earth and air
With thy voice is loud,
As, when Night is bare,
From one lonely cloud
The moon rains out her beams, and Heaven is over-
flowed.

7

What thou art we know not;
What is most like thee?
From rainbow clouds there flow not
Drops so bright to see,
As from thy presence showers a rain of melody.

8

Like a Poet hidden
In the light of thought,
Singing hymns unbidden,
Till the world is wrought
To sympathy with hopes and fears it heeded not:

9

Like a high-born maiden
    In a palace-tower,
Soothing her love-laden
    Soul in secret hour
With music sweet as love, which overflows her bower:

10

Like a glow-worm golden
    In a dell of dew,
Scattering unbeholden
    Its aërial hue
Among the flowers and grass, which screen it from the
    view:

11

Like a rose embowered
    In its own green leaves,
By warm winds deflowered,
    Till the scent it gives
Makes faint with too much sweet those heavy-wingèd
    thieves:

12

Sound of vernal showers
    On the twinkling grass,
Rain-awakened flowers,
    All that ever was
Joyous, and clear, and fresh, thy music doth surpass.

13

Teach us, Sprite or Bird,
    What sweet thoughts are thine:
I have never heard
    Praise of love or wine
That panted forth a flood of rapture so divine.

14

Chorus Hymeneal,
    Or triumphal chaunt,
Matched with thine would be all
    But an empty vaunt,
A thing wherein we feel there is some hidden want.

15

What objects are the fountains
    Of thy happy strain?
What fields, or waves, or mountains?
    What shapes of sky or plain?
What love of thine own kind? what ignorance of pain?

16

With thy clear keen joyance
    Languor cannot be:
Shadow of annoyance
    Never came near thee:
Thou lovest—but ne'er knew love's sad satiety.

17

Waking or asleep,
 Thou of death must deem
Things more true and deep
 Than we mortals dream,
Or how could thy notes flow in such a crystal stream?

18

We look before and after,
 And pine for what is not:
Our sincerest laughter
 With some pain is fraught;
Our sweetest songs are those that tell of saddest thought.

19

Yet if we could scorn
 Hate, and pride, and fear;
If we were things born
 Not to shed a tear,
I know not how thy joy we ever should come near.

20

Better than all measures
 Of delightful sound,
Better than all treasures
 That in books are found,
Thy skill to poet were, thou scorner of the ground!

21

Teach me half the gladness
    That thy brain must know,
Such harmonious madness
    From my lips would flow,
The world should listen then—as I am listening now.

Ode to the West Wind

1

O wild West Wind, thou breath of Autumn's being,
Thou, from whose unseen presence the leaves dead
Are driven, like ghosts from an enchanter fleeing.

Yellow, and black, and pale, and hectic red,
Pestilence-stricken multitudes: O thou,
Who chariotest to their dark wintry bed

The wingèd seeds, where they lie cold and low,
Each like a corpse within its grave, until
Thine azure sister of the spring shall blow

Her clarion o'er the dreaming earth, and fill
(Driving sweet buds like flocks to feed in air)
With living hues and odours plain and hill:

Wild Spirit, which art moving everywhere;
Destroyer and preserver; hear, oh, hear!

2

Thou on whose stream, mid the steep sky's commotion,
Loose clouds like earth's decaying leaves are shed,
Shook from the tangled boughs of Heaven and Ocean,

Angels of rain and lightning: there are spread
On the blue surface of thine airy surge,
Like the bright hair uplifted from the head

Of some fierce Maenad, even from the dim verge
Of the horizon to the zenith's height
The locks of the approaching storm. Thou dirge

Of the dying year, to which this closing night
Will be the dome of a vast sepulchre,
Vaulted with all thy congregated might

Of vapours, from whose solid atmosphere
Black rain, and fire, and hail will burst: oh, hear!

3

Thou who didst waken from his summer dreams
The blue Mediterranean, where he lay,
Lulled by the coil of his crystàlline streams,

Beside a pumice isle in Baiae's bay,
And saw in sleep old palaces and towers
Quivering within the wave's intenser day,

All overgrown with azure moss and flowers
So sweet, the sense faints picturing them! Thou
For whose path the Atlantic's level powers

Cleave themselves into chasms, while far below
The sea-blooms and the oozy woods which wear
The sapless foliage of the ocean, know

Thy voice, and suddenly grow grey with fear,
And tremble and despoil themselves: oh, hear!

4

If I were a dead leaf thou mightest bear;
If I were a swift cloud to fly with thee;
A wave to pant beneath thy power, and share

The impulse of thy strength, only less free
Than thou, O uncontrollable! If even
I were as in my boyhood, and could be

The comrade of thy wanderings over Heaven,
As then, when to outstrip thy skiey speed
Scarce seemed a vision; I would ne'er have striven

As thus with thee in prayer in my sore need.
Oh! lift me as a wave, a leaf, a cloud!
I fall upon the thorns of life! I bleed!

A heavy weight of hours has chained and bowed
One too like thee: tameless, and swift, and proud.

5

Make me thy lyre, even as the forest is:
What if my leaves are falling like its own!
The tumult of thy mighty harmonies

Will take from both a deep, autumnal tone,
Sweet though in sadness. Be thou, spirit fierce,
My spirit! Be thou me, impetuous one!

Drive my dead thoughts over the universe
Like withered leaves to quicken a new birth!
And, by the incantation of this verse,

Scatter, as from an unextinguished hearth
Ashes and sparks, my words among mankind!
Be through my lips to unawakened earth

The trumpet of a prophecy! O, Wind,
If Winter comes, can Spring be far behind?

To-morrow

Where art thou, beloved To-morrow?
   When young and old, and strong and weak,
Rich and poor, through joy and sorrow,
   Thy sweet smiles we ever seek,—
In thy place—ah! well-a-day!
We find the thing we fled—To-day.

from Hellas

Semichorus I

Life may change, but it may fly not;
Hope may vanish, but can die not;
Truth be veil'd, but still it burneth;
Love repulsed,—but it returneth!

(lines 34–37)

INDEX

OF TITLES

INDEX

OF FIRST LINES

147

About the Compiler

Leo Gurko is professor of English at Hunter College in New York City; he served as chairman of the department from 1954 to 1960. Educated at the College of the City of Detroit and at the University of Wisconsin, he is the author of TOM PAINE, FREEDOM'S APOSTLE and THE TWO LIVES OF JOSEPH CONRAD.

Dr. Gurko has worked as an advertising copy writer, translator, free-lance editor, and publisher's reader. He has made frequent radio and television appearances, and has written many articles on modern American literature.

He has spent two years in Europe: one with his family on a grant from the Ford Foundation, and the other on sabbatical leave. Among his avocations are tennis, travel, and the operas of Mozart and Verdi. He and his wife, herself an author of biographies for young readers, live in New York City with their children.

About the Illustrator

Lars Bo's leisure hours might be spent stalking deer in Scotland or wild boar in Alsace. Since he is married to a Scottish girl and lives in Paris, these regions are not as remote as they seem.

Mr. Bo is principally an engraver and watercolorist. He has seen several exhibitions of his work in Europe and, in 1965, traveled to the United States for a one-man showing in New York City. Although book illustration is a "secondary occupation" for Mr. Bo, he has worked on several adult books and received a prize for the best illustrated book in Copenhagen, Denmark, in 1960.

Lars Bo was born in Kolding, Denmark, and studied in Copenhagen at the Academy of Applied Arts. He was a member of the Danish Resistance from 1943 to 1945, and later came to Paris to study engraving and etching.